GREEN STAMPS FOR
HEAVEN

Copyright © Lissie Bean

Published by Chancing Lane Publishers

Paperback ISBN-13: 978-1-7397226-0-9
eBook ISBN-13: 978-1-7397226-1-6

Printed in the United Kingdom

All rights reserved in all media. No part of this publication may be reproduced, stored in retrieval system, copied in any form or by any means, electronic, mechanical, photocopying, recording or otherwise transmitted without written permission from the author and/or publisher. You must not circulate this book in any format. Any person who does any unauthorised act in relation to this publication may be liable to criminal prosecution and civil claims for damages

This book is a memoir. It reflects the author's present recollections of experiences over time. Some events have been compressed, and some dialogue has been recreated

Cover design and layout by www.spiffingcovers.com

Cover picture: Pattie circa 1951 with her first camera, an Eastman Kodak A.

Map illustration done by Julie Heathcote-Hacker.

GREEN STAMPS FOR
HEAVEN

LISSIE BEAN

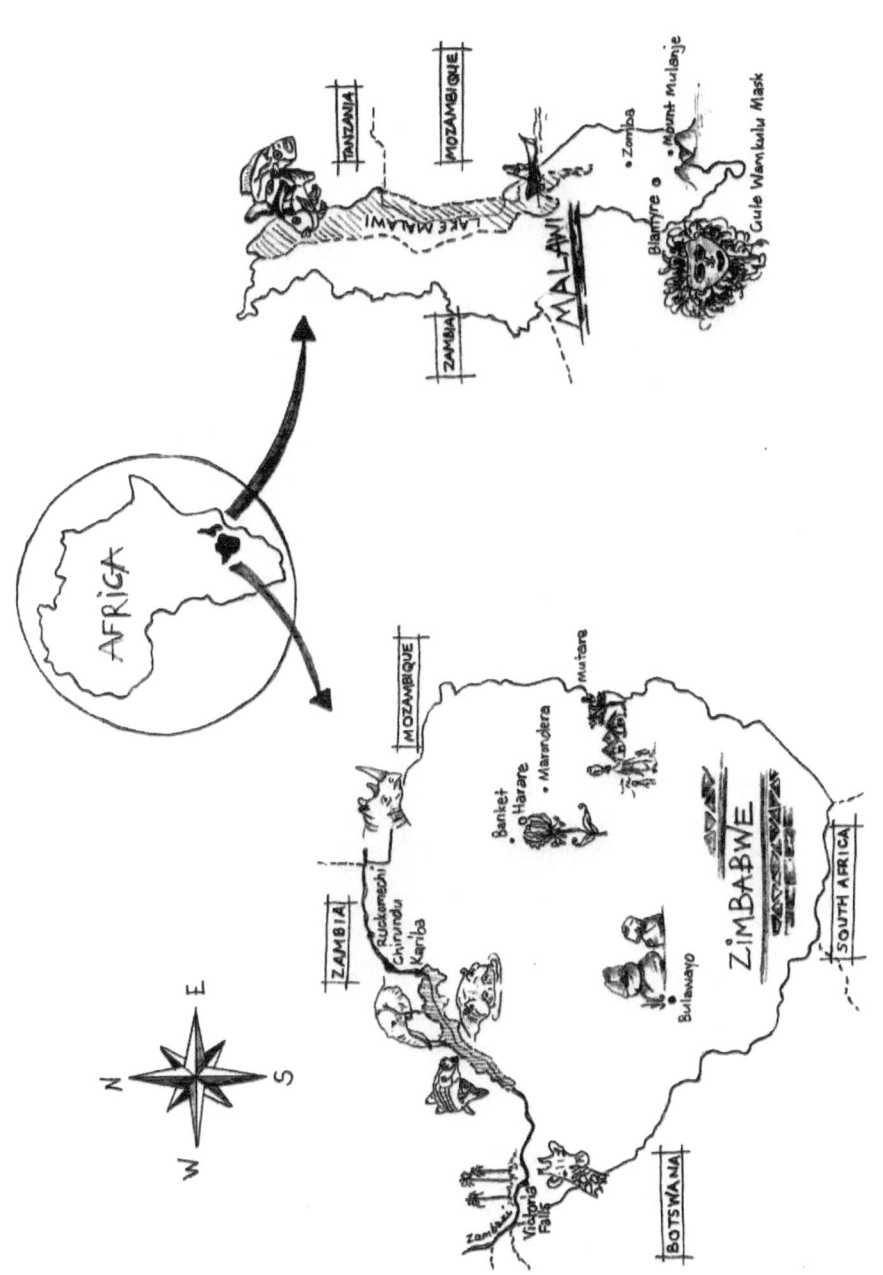

Contents

Introduction 9
Acknowlegements 11
Foreword 13
A Brief History 15

Chapter 1 19
Chapter 2 25
Chapter 3 35
Chapter 4 43
Chapter 5 51
Chapter 6 59
Chapter 7 69
Chapter 8 75
Chapter 9 83
Chapter 10 87
Chapter 11 91
Chapter 12 103
Chapter 13 109
Chapter 14 117
Chapter 15 123
Chapter 16 131
Chapter 17 137
Chapter 18 141

Chapter 19	147
Chapter 20	151
Chapter 21	157
Chapter 22	167
Chapter 23	171
Chapter 24	177
Chapter 25	181
Chapter 26	189
Chapter 27	195
Chapter 28	201
Chapter 29	209
Chapter 30	215
Chapter 31	223
Chapter 32	231
Chapter 33	239
Chapter 34	249
Chapter 35	259

INTRODUCTION

By Janet Wood
Chairperson of ZARDA
(Zimbabwe Alzheimer's and Related Disorders Association)
Tel: +263 242 494409
Email: zarda@zol.co.zw
Website: www.zarda.org

ZARDA is a support group, formed in 1998, for people with dementia and their families and friends. It is a registered Zimbabwean Welfare Organisation and a full member of Alzheimer's Disease International (ADI), which is based in London.

Our key objective is to give families, and other carers of affected persons, an opportunity to assist and encourage one another to share and discover information regarding the conditions of Alzheimer's and related mental disorders. Alzheimer's is one form of dementia that causes a progressive deterioration of the brain. Currently there are nine forms of dementia, which include Parkinson's, vascular dementia (post stroke) and Huntington's disease. Alzheimer's is the most common.

People need to realise dementia is a disease and not a normal part of ageing. There should be no stigma attached to it and love and support is essential for the patients and those whose task it is to care for them, as dementia affects the sufferer and impacts greatly on families, carers, communities, and societies on a local and international scale.

Sadly, we will all encounter someone with some form of dementia in our lifetime. This is a worldwide epidemic that is growing at an alarming rate. The international figures in 2010 showed there were 36 million people with dementia. In 2030 this figure will have risen to 66 million and in 2050, 115 million people with be suffering from this disease. An estimated 18 000 people in Zimbabwe are suffering from dementia and, by 2050, this figure is likely to rise to 27 000. We need to be prepared and gain as much knowledge as possible.

Working with Zarda has been a privilege and a source of inspiration to me on a personal level. Witnessing and sharing this journey with many individuals, long or short, I have been amazed at the courage, compassion and caring with which most people face this disease. Ageing can be associated with many losses, but none greater than from dementia, which gradually robs us of our ability to remember, to communicate and to function in all daily activities from the complex to the most basic. Most importantly, it robs us of our personalities and alters our behaviour. The challenge is to accept what cannot be changed. Coping with the trauma and sadness, however, develops strengths not previously recognised. I have the utmost admiration for those who are affected by dementia.

Green Stamps for Heaven is one such a story...

Janet Wood

ACKNOWLEGEMENTS

Norman Pink – Pattie's Knight in shining armour.

My sister, Christianne, your strength and courage made up for the lack of mine.

My partner, Jules, whose gentle heart and sense of humour made me laugh even in my darkest moments! I would never have finished this book without your love and support.

Vicki Rosedale, your Christian faith kept us on track, and your love for our family never faltered. You were, and always will be, our rock.

Dearest Aunty Mags, you patiently unveiled our family history and brought Pattie's childhood to life, without which this story would be incomplete.

Julie, my childhood friend who participated in most of my young adventures and never stopped believing I could put pen to paper.

Janis, Charmaine, Pat, Delia, Hildah, our friendship requires no words. You came running.

Debbie and Hans, you allowed Jules and me to go AWOL in the Ume.

I count myself lucky to have been surrounded by you all.

This book is dedicated to my mother, Patricia Shelagh Pink (1930-2017) and Vicki Angelene Rosedale (1961-2021).

FOREWORD

Surrounded by the beauty of Zimbabwe's Matusadona Wilderness, I started to write a book. I hadn't planned to, but frantic fingers pounded the keyboard searching for words to heal my angry heart, questioning myself, God, and anyone in the vicinity. My Mum, Pattie, loved the Matusadona area, then again, she loved the whole country. "How lovely!" I can hear her say. I sent her away when I could no longer cope with her illness. It was the right decision, sensible and all that, blah blah blah.

The more I wrote, the more I healed, and memories of happier times began to surface. Flashbacks of my delightful childhood and unforgettable moments with my mother. Recollections told to me by my grandparents, aunts and family friends, of a middle-class family who lived through both World Wars in England and witnessed independence in Malawi and Zimbabwe. Tales of toil, tribulation, love and adventure that have contributed to our family's soul.

Pattie had a smile that lit up a room. It was the only characteristic that endured throughout her battle with Alzheimer's disease. Every sufferer copes differently, some better than others, some longer, their families too. Overall, a huge amount of love, courage and respite is necessary to quell the helplessness. There is also - dare I say it - a humorous side to the illness, as acceptable behaviour shrinks into forgetfulness.

Writing about my own experience with the disease gave me the relief that I desperately needed and made sure that generations to come could read about Pattie's colourful life, a life she couldn't remember.

A BRIEF HISTORY

My maternal great-great-grandparents Wilhelm and Wilhelmine Stein left the municipality of Haenlein, Hesse in Germany, with their two sons, William and my great-grandfather, Franz. The family arrived in London, England in 1871 and opened a bakery in St Botolph which was considered relatively successful, employing seven staff members. In 1886 the family was granted citizenship by naturalisation. Wilhelm and Wilhelmine had a further five children, all of whom were born in Aldgate, London.

In 1890, aged 20, Franz married an 18-year-old London Irish woman called Winifred McDermott in Whitechapel. They had ten children, four girls and six boys who were all born in the boroughs of Islington and Holborn. Sadly, two of the girls died before their first birthday. Their fourth child, John Patrick was my grandfather. He was born in Islington in 1899.

In 1914 Britain entered World War I by declaring war on Germany. It was a difficult time for an immigrant family with German accents to be living in London. Whether it was through necessity or by choice, Wilhelm and Wilhelmine anglicised their names to William and Amelia. Franz became known as Francis, but he did not anglicize his surname to Steen like most of his male siblings had done. He worked long hours as a driver of a four-in-hand horse drawn coach and kept to himself, saying as little as possible to avoid his accent being detected.

At the start of the War, my grandfather, John Patrick

enlisted with the 6th City of London Rifles but was discharged for being underage at 15 years old. (Reg. No. 1374) He re-enlisted in 1916 and saw action in Gallipoli, France and Italy. At some point he was captured and sent to Giessen Prisoner of War camp in Hesse, Germany, (just over 200 kilometres from the town in which his grandparents were born). He remained tight-lipped about this time in his life and the information we have is sketchy. We do know that he worked in the camp hospital and escaped in 1917 with a piece of cloth which he had embroidered with the Royal Engineers badge for some unknown reason. He was demobbed in 1919 and returned home to Islington.

Post-war Britain was a hard place. Jobs created to repair the war damage had come to an end and unemployment had doubled from one to two million. Most of the unemployed were poverty stricken and those with jobs were asked to take pay cuts and work longer hours.

In the hope of finding better work and a better life, John Patrick left for Canada in 1921. On a return visit to England, he fell in love with a London-Irish woman called Veronica Delaney. He returned to Canada and frantically saved up for her boat fare. Somewhere between 1922 and 1925 John Patrick changed his surname from Stein to his mother's maiden name, McDermott. We don't know why, it's a family mystery. Perhaps it was to open more doors in post-war society or perhaps it was to sound more Irish to his fiancé's family.

Veronica arrived in Canada in 1926 and they were married at St Patrick's Church in Montreal, Quebec. "At last, she is mine!" John Patrick wrote to his brother after the wedding. By the following year, Veronica and John Patrick were ensconced in the Canadian Catholic community of Windsor, Ontario, and their first child, Maureen, was born within 18 months.

A year and a half later, they were crossing the new Ambassador Bridge back into Canada after a day trip to Detroit, when Veronica felt her waters break. It was the longest suspension bridge in the world and John Patrick felt every metre of it, hitting the accelerator and horn simultaneously to push through traffic in their Ford 8. He considered turning back to the closer American side, but with a twinkle in her eye Veronica convinced him to continue the same way.

Their second daughter, Patricia Shelagh, announced her arrival in the world with the lungs of an opera singer at 935, Church Street, Windsor, Ontario. It was clear from the beginning that she knew how to make an entrance and would've been disappointed not to have stopped traffic on the bridge!

The family returned to England in 1932 and Patricia was to become the second eldest of five girls - Maureen, Pattie, Veronica, Angela and Margaret. Sadly, they lost their twin brothers (Peter and Paul) when Veronica miscarried in 1940.

My Mum, Pattie, married Ken Bean in 1952 in Hampstead and after the birth of two sons the family moved initially to Southern Rhodesia before moving up to Nyasaland in 1961. They moved back to Rhodesia in 1968 and were divorced a decade later, after 25 years of marriage. In 1983, Pattie married Norman Pink in Zimbabwe. She opened a PR company and scripted, produced and presented over 60 documentaries for television and radio in Zimbabwe.

Pattie and Norman retired in England, having spent nearly 50 years in Africa.

1

Pattie was in her own world sitting in a wheelchair in the lounge refolding a pile of table napkins on her lap. She had no idea that she was about to leave Zimbabwe for good and had been dressed in her favourite gypsy skirt, red polo-neck sweater, warm socks and comfortable shoes for the journey.

Her makeup had been applied with ease, but her nails were painted with difficulty, fighting against her powerful grip on the table napkins. After a frantic search I found her dentures in the biscuit tin, they appeared to have munched their way through an entire packet of ginger nuts, but she popped them in without the usual fuss, smiled and looked beautiful. A black money pouch bulging with useless Zimbabwean billion-dollar notes dangled from her neck and a handbag stuffed with family letters was tucked into her side. Both were rarely out of her sight and touch them at your peril.

I wanted to wrap my arms around her, say I was sorry and tell her everything would be alright, but she usually mirrored my emotions which were building up to say goodbye. I kept my distance, loitering around the entrance to the lounge, watching her from afar.

Our dogs Scruffy and Muffin sensed the tension and barked for attention at her feet. In a little while, they would never see her again. To quieten them down, Vicki called them over to the couch where she was sitting reading from a small book of *Prayers for Daily Living*. Its bookmarked pages brimmed with guidance on attributes like patience and kindness which she would need escorting my mentally ill mother on a difficult

10-hour flight back to England.

Vicki had been a family friend for nearly 30 years and Pattie thought of her as a surrogate daughter. Her straightforward manner with religious undertones would keep Pattie calm during the flight. Compounded by a fear of flying, my frazzled emotions would reflect badly on Pattie creating the perfect environment for her to panic and have a major meltdown on board the plane. It was an acceptable excuse when I was so on edge and couldn't spend another minute yet alone ten hours on a flight quietening my mother's outcries for help; praising the manic folding of table napkins; responding to the incessant question, "Where's Lissie?" Me, the guilt-ridden yellow-bellied daughter shipping her out for a moment's peace and ever grateful to my loving friend for taking my place. Tears welled just looking at them both.

"You've got her sleeping pills, Vix? I asked, gulping back the tears. They'll help for a while."

She smiled and gave me two thumbs up, but Pattie instantly picked up on the sadness in my voice and became agitated.

"Help! Where's Lissie?" she cried.

"Look Mum, it's your favourite, Lukwesa Burak on the news" I answered quickly, trying to sound upbeat.

It was enough of a distraction to keep her calm, until the dangling black money pouch knocked a few napkins off her lap.

"Help! Quick! Quickers!" She yelled.

My partner Jules got to the floor before me and returned the napkins before Pattie had a chance to fully react. I wanted to scream but made nebulous conversation instead.

"Christianne can't wait to see you in Ipswich, Mum. Remember Joshua, Scott, and Ben, they've painted pictures for your room," I bungled.

I was asking her to remember something when her memory

was dying! Most names and places were meaningless. She couldn't remember any of her grandchildren yet alone the three in Ipswich. My sister, Christianne was counting the hours before Pattie's arrival, praying she would cope, where I had failed.

To avoid making any more stupid remarks, I scarpered to the kitchen and polished the tabletops for the umpteenth time until the gate bell finally rang. Our friends Janis and Charmaine had arrived for the airport run. I couldn't do that either. Janis cleared her throat and Charmaine shouted out a jolly hello from the driver's seat, both hiding the anguish of what was going to be a difficult farewell. Hearing the car engine, Pattie became agitated again.

"Quickers!" She screamed.

She was obsessive about going for rides in the car but unaware that this car was not just taking her around the block. It was taking her to the airport, and we were about to say goodbye in our driveway at home in Harare. It felt cruel and I wanted it over with but gathered the animals and everyone else for a photograph to mark the miserable occasion instead. Pattie's demeanour instantly changed when she spotted the camera. Shrieking with joy she posed with a smile and waved one of her crutches in the air to direct proceedings. It was instinct after decades as a TV presenter.

Hildah, our housekeeper, added to the furore by squeezing into the photograph at the last minute. Scruffy threw back his head and howled.

"Stop it Scruffy, it's only me, Hildah," she explained.

Hildah felt it necessary to constantly re-introduce herself to him because of his poor sight which made him bark even more. The louder he barked the more my mother guffawed into the camera. Our cats, Mac and Nyimo, got in on the action, meowing and swirling their tails around the tattered castors of the wheelchair, and just as Muffin plonked her toy onto Pattie's lap for a game, click! The last photograph of my mother in Africa was taken.

Vicki tapped her watch and Charmaine crept out of the lounge to collect the suitcase that I'd packed secretively all week. When Pattie heard the car engine for a second time she rocked her wheelchair into motion, determined not to miss out on a ride.

"Help! Quick, quickers!" She cried.

Deadpan, I wheeled her out to the driveway at speed. She scrambled into the front seat of the car with her table napkins and locked the door.

"Christianne will meet you at Heathrow," I gasped.

"Quickers! Where's Lissie?" she shouted out, looking straight at me.

"I'll see you soon, Mum," I choked.

"Why are you crying, darling?" She asked.

Her question caught me by surprise, she hadn't formed a full sentence in a while. Should I use her moment of clarity to explain again why she was being sent away? I'd feel better but she reacted badly the last time, marching around the garden with no concept of time, searching for exits, shouting for help. It would be unwise to risk the same episode before her flight.

"Because I love you," I replied, kissing her on the cheek.

"Help! Where's Lissie?" She yelled.

"I love you, Mum, I love you!"

She waved a red leather glove nonchalantly out of the window and didn't look back. The other glove had been squirreled away somewhere and wasn't found in time. I turned away when the car was out of sight and ran to her empty cottage at the bottom of our garden where the smell of Chanel No 5-perfume hung in the air and ginger biscuit crumbs lay scattered on the sideboard. When I found her missing red glove with a few other treasures under her pillow, I fell onto her bed and wailed uncontrollably. My mother was gone, never to return to her beloved Zimbabwe. Alzheimer's disease had broken her memory and my heart, but it wasn't always that way.

****

2

I had a rough night thinking about Pattie and Vicki and eventually woke Jules up at 4.30am to start packing the truck. Scruffy and Muffin followed us everywhere with their tails between their legs. They hated seeing our suitcases, but Hildah was pleased to be left in charge of the house and animals for a few days. The sun was barely up and Scruffy couldn't see a thing, but he could hear Hildah and started to bark.

"Stop it Scruffy, it's me Hildah," she responded.

By 4.45am we were on the road heading for the Ume River to celebrate Jules' sister's fiftieth birthday. The family was gathering for a long weekend at the crocodile farm where Debbie and her husband Hans lived and worked. A celebration of any sort felt undeserved, but the five-hour drive and 57-kilometre boat transfer across Lake Kariba, would take me far away from the memories at home and I couldn't get there fast enough. Clockwatching, it was now 6am in Zimbabwe, 5am in England. Vicki and Pattie would be flying across the English Channel, their journey almost at an end. Mine was just beginning.

A CD belting out the *Best of the Eighties* struggled to lift the mood in the twin cab. I lost my temper at the slightest thing and burst into tears when a battered Datsun station wagon slowed our progress going up the Great Dyke Mountain Pass. Billowing black exhaust smoke enveloped the old banger and the bottleneck of cars stuck behind it. When I managed to overtake on a short stretch, my filthy glare at the driver was reciprocated by murderous scowls from a small herd of fierce looking goats bleating from his back passenger seat. They lurched towards us when their vehicle swerved into our path and the driver smiled apologetically, waving a filthy rag which he was using to clear his windscreen of what I imagined was dreadfully smelly goats' breath.

"Lobola?" Jules asked, looking back to check the goats were alright.

In the Shona[1] custom, a man must pay his future in-laws a token of appreciation for his bride-to-be, which is known as a lobola. The larger the token, the greater the appreciation. If this was the case here, four goats would probably be a small part of the payment but judging by the danger that the driver was inflicting on himself and other roads, she must be a prize! At the height of her career Pattie would've chased the Datsun around the country just to get the full story and to capture film footage for future documentaries on topics like animal husbandry, Shona traditions or traffic safety.

We left the Datsun behind us in black cloud of exhaust smoke and sped past the farming towns of Lions Den and Karoi. At 8.30 my mobile phone pinged with a voice message from Vicki. Jules pressed the play button and I braced myself for a deluge of bad news, but Vicki only said three words, "arrived. Pattie fine." I could tell by her tone that she'd had a rough journey which I could do nothing about except hit the accelerator pedal harder and race towards the baobab tree lay-by on the Makuti-Kariba Road. A traditional place to stop for a drink poured from a well-stocked cooler box clattering on the back seat. By 10.00 we were sitting on a broken concrete bench, pouring a drink underneath an ancient baobab tree while keeping watch for wild animals that roamed the Kaburi Wilderness. The baobab tree was

---

1. Bantu ethnic group native to southern Africa, particularly Zimbabwe.

scratched with lifetimes of graffiti. Simple words and symbols memorialising love, life and death which I could have stared at all day, wallowing in self-pity, but we had a boat to catch.

Jules took over the driving for the last stretch and the winding roads of the Zambezi escarpment brought back memories of our last trip to the area when Pattie started behaving strangely. She would've arrived in Ipswich by now, and by the time we reached Lake Kariba an hour later, my mother and I were more than 12000 kilometres away from each other.

Excited staff stormed the car park to greet us. I left Jules shaking hands and skulked around to the back of the truck, where a cheerful boat captain stopped me from unpacking. He estimated a two-hour delay due to strong winds. The sky was blue but white horses danced on the water. It was the right decision to wait; Lake Kariba winds could be deadly. In no mood for polite conversation with fellow passengers I escaped to the shoreline, taking refuge behind an anthill conveniently located there.

The view of the Lake was spectacular and always took my breath away. A pair of Egyptian geese waddled along the shoreline, dodging the crashing waves. A couple of cormorants stood on a tree stump, taking advantage of the high winds to dry their outstretched wings. The cry of a fish eagle echoed in the horizon where my mind wandered for several hours until our travelling companions re-appeared on the shoreline, chattering with excitement because the transfer was going ahead. With daylight becoming a factor, the boat captain decided that the winds had died down sufficiently to attempt the crossing but warned the journey would be rough.

In a flurry of activity, suitcases, freezer boxes of meat, groceries, fishing rods, and people were loaded aboard the twin-engine speed boat. I could no longer avoid introductions and an American trader called Chuck, tilted his furry company cap at me.

"I hunt beevorrs, alligaytorrs, stawlts, sqeerrills and ottorrs for their hides," he roared in a Texan drawl, pointing at his gleaming alligator boots and belt.

Great, a hunter was trying to make friends.

"What a hero you are, you must be so proud wearing all those animal skins!" I snapped, squeezing his hand tightly.

My sarcastic comment whirled in the wind above the boat and a few passengers looked questioningly at me. I wasn't expecting to have tea with Brigette Bardot and understood that crocodile farming was a huge source of employment in the area, but my mood had found a target which Chuck could sense. Before I launched into a heated debate on animal farming, he clutched onto his fur hat and marched his alligator boots off to the front of the boat where he received a good walloping from the angry waves of the Nyami Nyami[2] river god, instead. Jules and I found a spot away from anyone else wearing skins and huddled together with white-knuckled grips on the railing. In turn receiving a good thrashing from Nyami Nyami for my sharp sarcastic tongue!

"Remember Debbie's first crossing to the Ume?" Jules shouted above the screaming boat engines.

Six months ago, Hans was taking Debbie across the Lake to the Ume for the first time with their three small dogs and their housekeeper, Fatima. A violent storm blew over forcing them to take shelter on the shores of a tiny island for the night. Clothing from Debbie's suitcase was distributed for warmth but the only item big enough for Hans was his wife's pink floral dressing gown. Once the storm had passed, he searched the island for dry wood and photographs of him trying to light a small fire in his colourful garb, were sent with

---

2. Important god to the Tonga people, believed to protect and give sustenance to people in the area.

a smiley face emoji around the globe.

Thankfully we managed to escape an island sleepover with the animal traders on board our boat and arrived at the calm waters of the Ume River, bruised and weather-beaten. After a three-hour wind bashing, Jules' mop of curly brown hair was the shape of a weathervane, pointing west. My hair had been blown into a useful frontal horn that was poised to jab at conversation makers trying to take advantage of the puttering boat engines.

As we approached land the harbour gradually came to life and fellow passengers were pointing out animals in every direction but most of the chatter on board was conveniently drowned out by the loud clicking sound of cicada beetles in the treeline. It was mating season for the superfamily of bugs and the noise from their drumming tymbals hit the boat in voluminous waves. Scanning the shoreline, I could see daredevil plover birds darting into the open mouths of sunbathing crocodiles, flossing bits of decaying meat from their jaws. A herd of elephants plodded towards the treeline for the night, their legs darkened from an evening swim. Hippos splashed about in the water but the pod nearest to our boat swivelled ominously in our direction. Having experienced a hippo attack in my teens I was extremely wary of them and watched their every move until we passed by. As dusk settled over this beautiful land, I breathed in the scent of the African bush and the pungent smell of potato trees, whose branches beckoned us off the water to safety.

Suddenly the engines revved up and the boat swung hard right. Passengers teetered and snatched back at the railing searching for a cause. The captain had decided to turn the boat away from the darkening jetty and rammed it into the shoreline next to a well-lit pumphouse instead. The heavy boat stopped short of land with crocodile-infested waters below, which didn't appear to bother anyone but me.

A tall man wearing green work overalls and a large, sun-bleached floppy hat waved at us with both hands from the shore. He caught the guy rope and wrapped it several times around an old tractor tyre while my travelling companions jumped to land, including Chuck who had already drawn a crowd with his alligator boots.

Old sports injuries to my knees made any sort of leap impossible so I hatched a plan to lower myself into the water from the boat railing and wade to shore, hopefully with some speed. Fortunately, Hans appeared before I took the plunge and, after a quick explanation from Jules, he sloshed through the water to my rescue, leaving Bushy, his liquorice-coloured mongrel, spinning in circles of excitement on the shoreline.

"Lower yourself onto my shoulders," he commanded.

"I'm heavy, Hans."

"Now! These waters are dangerous," he said, turning his back to the boat.

He muffled a few Afrikaans[3] expletives when I sat down on the bow and slumped onto his shoulders like a sack of potatoes. With flip flops in one hand, my free hand clawed into his chest while my backside waved goodbye to the boat captain. Not the entrance or departure I'd planned, but Bushy enjoyed it, giving me a good sniff as Hans dumped me on land.

"We must hurry," he said, stretching his back and glancing up at the last of the sun. "It's quite a walk to your lodge and there are lions and buffalo in the area."

The man in the floppy hat understood the urgency and came skidding to a halt with a rusty Monarch wheelbarrow.

"My name is Mistake. Which is your luggage?" He asked with a smile.

Pointing out the suitcases, fishing rods, crates of drinks

---

3. West Germanic language spoken in South Africa.

and a hefty tin trunk of groceries, I enquired how he got his unusual name.

"It's better you speak to my mother," he said with another smile.

Judging by the speed of his response, he'd been asked the question many times and I immediately had visions of his mother swearing in Tonga[4] at the quivering sire as their unplanned baby entered the world. Hans thought it would be a good idea for Mistake go to the registry office when he turned 21 and change his name defiantly to *Not-a-mistake!* I agreed with him as he seemed like a lovely man.

"Thank you, Mistake," I said, despite it sounding odd to me.

"You're welcome," he yelled, running off down a dirt road with his laden wheelbarrow.

We formed an obedient line behind Hans in preparation for the walk to our lodge. His senses were on high alert listening out for wild animals which would be hungry at this time of the day. My urban-trained ears could pinpoint a flailing generator coughing through the nightly power outages in Harare but struggled when it came to identifying dangers of the African bush. Every bump and crackle sent adrenaline firing through my veins, which Hans found amusing, particularly when I squealed after a dubious mopane leaf landed on my shoulder. Jules went mute when a twig fell from a branch and she started communicating with wide eyes, raised eyebrows and sharp jabs into my ribs. Repeated jabs were launched when the dirt road shrank into a footpath and Hans casually told us about an angry buffalo bull that had charged him from the Jesse[5] bush near Kipling's Guest Lodge. He had escaped with minor injuries

---

4. Bantu language of the indigenous Batonga tribe who live in the Zambezi Valley
5. A deciduous straggling shrub.

by dodging around a few mopane trees. I was eyeballing the closest clump of trees when something crackled in the bush to our right and a wood pigeon took flight looking just as terrified as me.

Hans tutted my silliness and forged ahead but I struggled to keep up with dodgy knees and ill-chosen flip flop shoes. Each jab from Jules' set off more alarm bells and noisy ridges of sand crunched under my feet making stealth mode virtually impossible. Nature film images of laggers being eaten first were top of mind when Bushy froze and Hans signalled for silence, pointing out hippopotamus footprints on the ground.

"Be very quiet," he whispered.

I slipped onto tiptoes without taking a breath until Hans gave us the signal to continue but the hard plastic flip flop strap pinched between my toes and hurt like hell.

"Are we nearly there Hans?" I pleaded.

"Shush," he whispered, turning around with a powerful stare.

As we got closer to the water, the path muddied and cut through dense Jesse bush. I could hear hippos tearing up grass with their teeth but knew sound carried a long way in the bush and tried not to overreact. The wet ground silenced my crunching slops, but thick mud stuck to the soles, doubling their weight and suctioning my feet to the ground where one of Africa's most dangerous animals was having an evening nibble.

To make matters worse, sticky spider webs criss-crossed the Jesse bush at the perfect height for my horned hairdo to scoop them up in spades. I tried not to become hysterical and continued stumbling along the path, quietly swiping wildly at the bungee jumping spiders under my nose, until Bushy stopped again. With one paw in the air, he growled into the darkness where the sound of snapping branches was getting louder. Another round of rib jabs from Jules almost punctured a lung and I wanted to be a sack of potatoes again, back on Hans' shoulders, minus my ridiculous flip flops which would've hopefully been lost to the mud in my leap.

"You're welcome," shouted Mistake, squeezing past us to collect another load.

Hans had identified the sound of an incoming wheelbarrow well in advance and chuckled at our pasty looking faces but picked up the pace none-the-less. He rushed us past the hippo and buffalo danger zones, up an embankment and around an enormous anthill. We were almost jogging by the time we reached a wire mesh fence where he opened the gate to our lodge and shut it quickly behind us.

A man dressed in chef's whites was standing under the back door light, surrounded by our luggage and an enthusiastic swarm of sticky moths. Walking towards us, he extended his hand.

"My name is Wonder. I am your cook," he said with a warm smile.

It was clear how his parents felt when he was born so there was no need to ask how he got his fantastic name. Jules' niece, Charn, and her boyfriend, Adam, rushed out the door to greet us. They had arrived the day before and whisked us around the lodge with much excitement revealing all the attributes of our holiday home.

The kitchen was offset from an open plan reception room which had a four-piece lounge suite, vintage sideboards and a teak dining room table and chairs. A large single bedroom with a separate bathroom and toilet came off the passageway and terracotta floor tiles flowed out onto a wide veranda with an abundance of garden furniture. A pine stairway led up to two ensuite doubles upstairs, each at opposite ends of the lodge. Charn walked us into our bedroom and straight to the balcony where the views were curtained by night skies. She couldn't wait for us to see how spectacular they would be in the morning and started naming all the different animals she had spotted when Adam shouted up to us that dinner was served.

We followed her back downstairs and cheered as Wonder placed a chicken curry of restaurant quality on the table. Sitting next to a drink's tray, below a wobbly ceiling fan we told Charn and Adam an exaggerated version of our long journey to the Ume River. Smelly goats' breath, "alligaytorr" boots, *Not-a-mistake*, buffalo bull and bungee jumping spiders. Apart from a knowing touch from Charn, no one mentioned Pattie, but I left for bed before alcohol and sadness had a chance to gel.

Our room had an enormous bed that was wrapped tightly in mosquito netting and pushed up against a red brick wall. Sturdy teak rafters held up a thatched roof without a ceiling and polished pine flooring creaked with every step. Nightjars and bats swooped in like fighter jets from the open balcony targeting insects fluttering around a side light. Hoping they'd all disperse I turned off the light and unpacked in moonlight. Fumbling around in my suitcase Pattie's bag of lost treasures fell out and pinched a nerve. For some torturous reason I'd stuffed it in at the last minute. After sharing a fitful bath with some unusual insects, I fought my way under the mosquito net and into bed. From my cocoon, I watched the stars blinking around the moon and listened to night apes chattering in symphony with owls and frogs. I thought about Christianne's first tumultuous night with Pattie in Ipswich and covered my head with the sheet.

****

3

Tiny cubes of sun drops squeezed through the mosquito net tickling my eyes open. I'd had the best night's sleep in months and nothing, but nature's sounds filled the room. It was peaceful, too peaceful, where was Pattie? Bolting upright with fright I wormed my way out of my cocoon and metamorphosed into a fluttering bride with a crooked veil, scattering insect carcass confetti in a trail towards the balcony. As I leant over the wooden railing the veil slipped off my crown and a gecko jerked from its sunny spot, eyeballing my invasive elbow and a sticky moth that had somehow pinned itself to my horned hairdo like a fascinator.

Below the balcony, a bright green lawn glistening with morning dew, rolled around pretty rockeries and flowerbeds down to a diamond mesh fence, only metres away from the river. An inviting glitterstone swimming pool and waterfall sparkled with sunlight attracting colourful dragonflies to the edge for a morning drink. At the bottom of the garden a chorus of go-away-birds and hornbills pecked at a generous canteen of fruit provided by an enormous fig tree and a cluster of palms.

Charn was right, the view was magnificent. As far as the eye could see daylight had transformed night skies into a glorious panorama of African wilderness. Through the fence, I could see hippos wallowing in the river, blowing bubbles and whirling their tails, sounding less menacing than they had on our walk the previous evening. Several were grazing on land and every step of their size 13 feet suctioned up fresh mud, unearthing bugs for the cattle egrets to eat. A lonely kingfisher sat arched on a fossilised mopane tree that was pegged into the Ume River which swirled with life. Across the water, the Matusadona mountains rose from clouds of bushfire smoke and from within its folds the call of the fish eagle caught the wind and celebrated the beauty of Africa.

It was an incredible way to start the day and the warmth of the sun seemed to soothe my worries about Pattie. I needed to get hold of Christianne and find out if by some small chance, there was any good news, but it was too early to phone England. In the meantime, I had a few pressing emails to answer and crept out of the room with my laptop and the bag of Pattie's lost treasures, leaving Jules to sleep.

The creak of the wooden stairs brought Wonder out from the kitchen, dressed again in his chef's whites. He had been up for hours, stoking the boiler for hot water and preparing a marvellous breakfast to show off his cooking prowess. The dining room table had been laid and flasks of tea and coffee stood beside a wicker basket of rusks. Mouth-watering wafts of bacon, egg and toast emanated from an old hostess trolley. Each display was adorned with sprigs of orange bougainvillea for that Michelin touch.

Out of habit I found myself whispering "good morning" so that Pattie couldn't hear me. It usually added a few extra peaceful minutes before the daily onslaught. Wonder whispered back out of politeness and explained that Charn and Adam had walked across to Debbie and Hans to join the rest of the family for breakfast. Debbie's two other daughters had arrived for the celebration: Paula and her husband Brad with their two-year-old son Jordan, and Hayley with her husband Bruce. Hans had taken the men tiger fishing at the crack of dawn leaving the girls behind to catch up on Hayley's recent announcement that she was pregnant with her first child.

Wonder looked disappointed when I by-passed the food trolley but helped move a bamboo table to the veranda with a clear view of the river. While my laptop booted up, I got comfortable on a garden chair and opened the bag of Pattie's lost property. Inside it was a red leather glove, an empty Chanel No 5-perfume box and an old diary. They were my mother's treasures, and I was sorry that they had been left behind.

"I need to write a book about my mother," I blurted out, surprising myself.

"You are a writer, Madam?" Wonder asked.

"I have a painting and decorating business; my mother was sick, but Jules is a teacher." I answered quickly, knowing this would give me more credence in his culture.

The need to write had come out of the blue. I was grieving for my mother, yet she was still alive, I was angry with God for letting her become sick and haunted by my failings. After answering the emails, it was still too early to phone England, so I opened a blank Word document, fully expecting words to flow in a torrent of self-justification. None came. It was easier to stare out at the Ume River and dunk several enormous rusks into a mug of tea.

Pattie used to say that "a cup of tea fixes everything". Years ago, it had been her only response when I announced that I might be pregnant. It was a few nights before leaving for university in South Africa and my timing couldn't have been worse. Of course, a cup of tea wouldn't fix this, but when a strong cup was poured, we'd sit down and discuss the best way forward. The larger the problem, the larger the cup. Big mugs came out on that occasion. Fortunately, it was a false alarm and after a lengthy discussion on better contraception, that was that!

The memory spurred my fingers on to bash out one

word, - Pattie. Not exactly a eureka moment but seeing my mother's name on the screen triggered a flood of pent-up tears, blurring my vision making it impossible to write anything else. Thankfully, the thatched A-frame roof of the lodge went down to the ground and hid my sadness from Wonder.

"Get over yourself!" I sniffed.

An hour later the same word glared at me from the screen next to a mounting pile of tissues and an empty bowl of rusks. I was on the verge of hyperventilation when the sudden sound of hooves, tap-tapping on the glitterstone tiles behind the thatch, booted self-pity into touch and survival mode kicked in.

I knew that any wild animals with hooves couldn't eat me, but they could trample me to death or gouge out a few body parts with their horns. Had the angry buffalo bull somehow got in? Perhaps an eland had jumped the two-metre-high fence that kept the grounds of the lodge safe? Africa's largest antelope certainly had the ability to do that and could do some damage with its dangerously long horns.

While brainstorming all sorts of scenarios I leant backwards in my chair fully expecting some life-threatening creature to charge but I zoomed in to a small flock of seven sheep instead. They trotted confidently past my desk and started bleating "catch-me-if-you-can" loudly to any predators that might be on the prowl outside the fence. Without a care in the world, they dodged the garden furniture and fell to their knees for a morning drink at the swimming pool. Only the twin lambs appeared a little jittery, jumping aside each time the pool vacuum cleaner gurgled menacingly on the steps.

Wonder explained that they were Hans' small breeding herd, and that lamb roast was a real treat in the Ume - especially for the important guests at Kipling's Lodge, like Chuck. It was enough of a reason for another meltdown and

Wonder rocked awkwardly from foot to foot as I offloaded my mother's story. An occasional 'eish'[6] from below his bowed head affirmed his sympathy, but he too, couldn't understand why I'd sent her away, which didn't help. I sensed his relief when Jules came bounding down the stairs in full St Francis of Assisi mode, demanding an explanation about lamb roasts.

"We can adopt them, send money for food every month," she declared.

It was a daft idea, but we felt better. Wonder simply nodded to appease his strange new guests, especially when Jules started giving the sheep names. Sturdy Sergio, Grumpy Edith, Randy Ralph, Sassy Gertrude, Saucy Cindy, and twin lambs, Shawn and Stewart were oblivious to our plans to rescue them from the butcher's knife.

Edith was the fearless matriarch. After finishing her drink at the pool, she approached my desk stamping her foot with determination to get food for her family. She bleated at me in a gravelly tone revealing a large gap between her two very intimating front teeth. Her nostrils flared like balloons when she spied a corner of a rusk next to my laptop but was diverted from a raid when Jules scattered a few pieces of toast, making sure each sheep got a morsel. Sassy Gertrude tapped towards me on pointe searching for crumbs. She was the glamorous chick on the block with long eyelashes and mascaraed eyes. Only a lack of nail varnish on her elegant hooves and a splash of ruby red on her lips let her down. I tried to hand-feed her a bit of toast, but it was too soon in our relationship for her to take it from me.

Shawn and Stewart were attacking a bed of arum lilies, when Edith spied Mistake carrying a heavy bowl on his

---

6. An informal word used to express a range of emotions from surprise to resignation.

head. The load squashed his oversized floppy hat down over his eyes, highlighting a smile. He released one hand to wave good morning, spilling food pellets onto the lawn and Edith immediately summoned her flock into formation with a deep growl. Gertrude sashayed to the back row, and they all followed the food trail to the bottom of the garden for breakfast. After sending Christianne a quick text message I followed Jules to the hostess trolley but was too full of rusks to eat anything more.

Wonder looked disappointed again but perked up when I helped him unpack our enormous tin trunk of groceries into the pantry. He carefully married each item to the A4 menu sheet that was inside and made a point of putting the potatoes, rice, and maize meal back into the trunk, "safe from the rats and mice". There was an enormous amount of food. As far as we knew there weren't any shops nearby and we didn't want to go short on our first self-catering holiday with Charn and Adam. We would be grateful for the excess later, but I couldn't help feeling that Wonder thought it decadent.

By midday my message to Christianne still hadn't gone through and I was relieved when Mistake arrived to escort us to Debbie and Hans' cottage for lunch where I might have better luck with the signal. He loaded our cooler box onto his wheelbarrow, and we followed him down the same path as yesterday but turned right at the harbour. The cottage was only about a kilometre away, but far enough to feel vulnerable walking through the Jesse bush. Hugging the mopane treeline Jules and I started to giggle and broke into a run the closer we got to their gate. Mistake thought this was hilarious and chased after us with the wheelbarrow, kicking up dust and grunting like an angry buffalo bull.

Hans and Debbie had transformed an ordinary Rhodesiana cottage into a beautiful character home with feature walls, hanging baskets and metal ornaments. A derelict boat hull overflowed with petunias and enormous clay pots spilled with yellow and white daisies. The view of the water was spectacular, but Debbie felt it was spoiled by a bushy island too close to shore. She teased Hans about trimming "that" hedge to fix "her" view.

Sitting around their splash pool with our feet in the water, Hans explained that the mobile signal was dreadful in the area, and that I just had to persist with it. Jules brought up the subject of the sheep and Debbie thought the names were fabulous, but Hans remained non-committal about future roast dinners. He changed the subject with news that lions had killed another buffalo in the Ume Conservancy during the night. I asked what hungry creatures might be attracted by the delicious smells of the boerewors[7] that he was cooking on the braai[8] and he tut-tutted at my silliness.

The banter cheered me up enormously, but the need to speak to my sister weighed heavily on my mind. Straight after lunch Mistake walked me through the Jesse bush and back to our lodge at speed.

****

---

7. Traditional Afrikaans spicy sausage.
8. Afrikaans word for a barbeque.

4

I walked down to the fig tree where the sheep were having an afternoon snooze. Edith barely lifted her head and was totally unmoved by my outcries about the bad mobile signal in the area. After walking the plot, I returned to my desk annoyed and relieved that I hadn't got through to Christianne.

Shuffling through Pattie's bag of lost treasures again I pulled out her *Charles Letts's Schoolgirl's Diary* and rubbed the cover as she would have done 67 years ago when she received it. The musty pages revealed faint information pencilled in by my mother as a teenager during the Second World War and presented me with the perfect place to start her story. Eureka!

The inside cover displayed a map of the British Empire, overwritten with an inscription - *To Patricia, with love from Mrs Meredith, Whitchurch, Brecon.* Pattie wrote her own address down as *'Springfield', Alexandra Road, Brecon,* followed by a notation on her family members: *Mommy and daddy - Veronica and John Patrick McDermott. Sisters - Maureen, Veronica (Bin), Angela, and Margaret.* Her sister Veronica had the unusual nickname of *Bin,* which was the name of Margaret's childhood fantasy friend and saved confusion with their mother's name. Pattie noted that her father, John Patrick, called them all his *"treasures".*

My mother and my aunts had retold stories of this period in their lives so many times that they were etched into our family history, and I hoped to remember them correctly.

The McDermott's lived in Highgate, London, where Bin,

Angela, and Margaret attended La Sainte Union Catholic School, and their older sisters Maureen and Pattie went to St Ursula's Convent School. At the start of the Second World War, Veronica and her five girls were evacuated from Paddington Station to the home of Lady Gompertz in Mayfield, Sussex. They were lucky that children under the age of five had to be accompanied by their mothers. A Kindertransport[9] child called Gillian also lived with them there, but the little girl never spoke a word. They always felt sorry for her, having been sent from Germany, without her family, to live in a foreign country with strangers who didn't speak her language.

In June 1940, John Patrick's brother, Lance Corporal Vincent Steen of the Royal Corps of Signals (Reg. No. 2563335) went missing in action. A month later they found out that he had been killed in Dunkirk and was buried in Lille, France. His mother died shortly afterwards; of a broken heart, so they said.

After France was occupied by the Nazis, it was only a matter of time before Britain was attacked from across the English Channel. The Battle of Britain began in July 1940 and Germany subjected Great Britain to a long series of bomb attacks from the air. On a summer's day, Pattie and her sisters were walking to church, glistening in their church whites when they were rushed at by an armed British soldier. He dragged them to safety under a truck, just before a Luftwaffe aircraft swooped down with guns firing. Veronica was perturbed to see her children arriving at church covered in engine grease but was ever grateful to the soldier when she realised what had happened. Pattie and Bin were again strafed by enemy aircraft while walking home from school

---

9. Organised rescue of predominantly Jewish children from Nazi Germany, Austria, Czechoslovakia, and Poland, and their placement in British foster homes.

and survived by diving into a ditch.

It was a stressful time for Veronica keeping her five children safe while witnessing daily dogfights in the skies above the Sussex coastline. Her beloved John Patrick remained in London and Veronica prayed for his safety when German bombs rained down on the town during the Blitz. She miscarried twin boys who she called Peter and Paul and John Patrick drove all day to be with her. They watched the swoops and dives of a crippled RAF plane coming towards them from the lounge window. It missed Lady Gompertz's house by a whisker and crashed at the end of the road. John Patrick rushed to the scene and managed to say the Lord's prayer before the pilot passed away.

When it became too dangerous to remain on the coast, Veronica and her girls were moved further west, where the German planes couldn't reach. Maureen and Patricia returned to London briefly to be evacuated with their school. Every pupil from St Ursula's Convent was labelled and sent by train to Brecon in Wales. Veronica and her three youngest girls were despatched to the home of Mrs Morgan, also in Brecon. She was a reluctant host and the billeting officer had to put his foot in the door to stop her from shutting them out. Maureen and Pattie joined them when school closed for the holidays, which meant Mrs Morgan had six extra bodies in her home: Catholic ones, at that. She was a fundamentalist Presbyterian and didn't speak to Veronica for weeks after catching her knitting on a Sunday! The girls were provided with warm beds and a safe home but most of the interaction only occurred in the shared kitchen when Veronica cooked her own food rations.

Their neighbour, Mrs Meredith, was much more amenable towards the girls. She gave them her collection of Charles Dickens books to read and invited them round regularly to make pancakes for tea and to take her spaniel,

Bill, for walks. In 1944 she gave Pattie the gift of the *Charles Letts's Schoolgirl's Diary* that I was reading.

The first 50 pages of the diary held pre-printed information that was considered useful to a teenager at the time. Multiplication tables; helpful hints for young ladies at work and play; careers for women; logarithms; books to read; principal French irregular verbs; German strong verbs; countries of the world and, of course, a map of the British colonies. It was demanding stuff.

Under a section on *Careers for Women*, Pattie had circled the words *civil service* and did the same on page seven around the word *journalism*. Had my mother dreamt of working as a civil servant or journalist for the British Empire across the seas? According to the diary, a third-class officer in the Ministry of Labour earned £225 a year. Mrs Meredith paid two shillings for the diary, so £225 must have seemed a fortune. Pattie frequently summarised her savings on the inside back cover, £5/13 shillings in November 1943, £6 in January 1944 and, by the 23rd of June 1945, she had accumulated £7/10.

Historic British sporting achievements were pre-printed in the diary, for prosperity. They noted that Miss A. Marble had won the England Lawn Tennis championship in 1939. In 1943, Oxford beat Cambridge in the boat race by two thirds of a length in a time of four minutes and 49 seconds. England beat Scotland 12-2 in the 1939 Women's Lacrosse. The English Women's Hockey team beat Scotland 4-2 at the Kennington Oval. Some fixtures were left blank having been uncontested in wartime.

The section on *Books to read - especially for girls* included thrilling stuff like Mary Thomas' *Embroidery Book*, Cornelia Meigs' Story of Louisa Alcott and Jean Stewart's *301 Things a Bright Girl Can Do!*

Under personal memoranda, Pattie wrote that she had

size 3 shoes, size 6¼ gloves, size 6¾ hat, she was five foot four inches tall, and weighed five stone, thirteen pounds. Her school timetable included maths, Latin, art, needlework, French, geography, science, music, and games. Exam results scrawled onto page 49 revealed a popular, diligent student who liked her teachers and excelled in games and art.

A section on *Safety for Cyclists* warned a young lady *"never to lose control of her bicycle by riding too quickly downhill or to ride with feet on handlebars, or with no hands"*. I imagined Pattie freewheeling down the Brecon hills, with her size three feet on the handlebars holding onto the hat on her head with her small, gloved hands, breaking every rule in the book!

She went to church every Sunday, confession and Benediction in the evening and had elocution lessons on Saturday mornings. What little time she had left, she went to youth club and took Bill for walks on the heath. Playing bagatelle with *"daddy,"* when he visited once a month from London in his Ford 8, was a cause for great excitement.

Birthdays and presents were uncomplicated and modest. She gave her sister, Margaret a prayer book on a snowy day in February and looked forward to the Eisteddfod preliminaries at half term, where she won first prize for art and third for composition. In May, Bin celebrated her twelfth birthday with a picnic and Pattie went bathing, mushroom and blackberry picking for her fourteenth birthday in September. The same week, she was made games captain and selected as goalkeeper for first team hockey, which I found amazing for someone so small!

The diary also revealed that Pattie's interest in film began at a young age. She visited The Palace Theatre every Wednesday, Friday, and Saturday during the heyday of cinema, when movies were inexpensive to watch and ran throughout the day. The list of films she saw included: Errol

Flynn and Bette Davies in *The Sisters* and *Springtime in the Rockies; The Irish in Us* with James Cagney and Pat O'Brien; and Bette Davies in *The Petrified Forest*. The list continued over the page: *Sierra Sue, Dear Octopus, Coney Island, Slightly Dangerous, Snow White and the Seven Dwarfs, Thunderbird,* Bing Crosby in *Dixie, The Great Waltz, Sky's the Limit, Stormy Weather, The Drum, Hallo Frisco Hallo, Jitterbug, Four Feathers, Gentleman Jim, Yellow Canary, Stage Door Canteen, Serenade of the West, Sweet Rosie O'Grady, Road to Zanzibar,* and *The Strange Death of Adolf Hitler.*

Her last entry noted that she went to midnight Mass, had turkey dinner on Christmas day, received a watch from *"daddy and mommy,"* and a parcel of candy, chewing gum and socks from her Uncle Augustine in Canada.

****

I closed the little diary just in time for the rumble of a motorbike to divert my thoughts. Hans tooted the horn and Jules shouted out from the back seat that it was fishing time. Time to catch my first big tiger fish, and the Ume River teemed with them! Bushy seemed just as excited, barking alongside the wheels.

After gathering all the fishing equipment pronto, we followed Mistake to a small gate at the bottom of the garden where Hans had moored a fishing boat earlier that day. Edith spotted the cooler box on Mistake's head, and thinking that it was her food, growled her flock into line.

"It's not for you, Edith," Mistake explained.

Edith wasn't dissuaded easily. If not for a scattering of crisps at the gate from Jules, the entire flock would've followed the cooler box onto the boat and joined us fishing.

At 12 years old, Bushy's hips were failing, but somehow,

he always reached the boat first. After a lift from Hans, he moved straight to his favourite position under the driver's console as Mistake pushed the boat off into the river shouting "tight lines!"

Hans steered towards Bird Island, which was aptly named and apparently the perfect spot for tiger fishing. One side of the island was relatively shallow where a pod of hippos spent the day wallowing. The other side had a deep channel favoured by tiger fish. The trick was to tie the boat up at the point where both levels met and catch bream in shallows to use as tiger fish bait in the channel.

Within minutes of casting, Jules caught the first bream and Bushy leapt up from under the console, barking and thumping his tail loudly on the hull. Most of Bird Island emptied and the hippos swivelled in our direction. The raucous continued while Hans reached for the tackle box to use as a chopping board. With a single stroke from his Rambo knife, he sliced off the fish head, sideswiping it into the water and cut the fillet into dainty strips. Bushy stopped barking once he'd received the first sliver of fish. It was tradition between this man and his dog.

Our keep net filled quickly with bream, but Bushy's excitement started to irritate the hippos and Hans had to move each time one got too close. We had yet to put a tiger trace in the water when a hippo dived towards us leaving me to wonder if it would pass by or take a chunk out of the boat from underneath. Hans eventually responded to my pleas to move from Bird Island altogether. He drove to deeper water where it felt a lot safer and tied the boat up to a tree stump as the sun went down over the Bumi Hills. It was magnificent, but the tiger fishing was awful.

The family were having sundowners on the veranda when we got back. The boys had caught several large tiger fish, but we'd caught enough bream to change the dinner menu to fish and chips, fresh Kariba bream was a meal not to be missed. I left them all discussing favourite cooking methods and walked down to the fig tree but still couldn't get hold of Christianne.

****

5

My writing desk had been polished by the time I came downstairs at five o' clock the next morning. The wicker basket had been replenished with rusks and a side plate of toast for the sheep had been added to the display - tokens of support from Wonder in my quest to write or to avoid another meltdown. I had a couple of hours to do either before the rest of the lodge stirred.

Wonder was in the pantry, counting the potatoes in the tin trunk to make sure future meals had not been skewed by the impromptu fish and chips dinner last night. After agreeing that there was more than enough left, he secured the lid and the words *Ken Bean, Zomba, Nyasaland* in chipped white enamel paint, caught my eye. *Nyasaland* had been hastily crossed out and replaced by the word *Malawi*. The tin trunk had been in our family for at least 40 years but suddenly seemed more poignant because I was writing a book.

"That's my father," I pointed out to Wonder.

He expected another long story, but I decided to write it down instead. Gertrude almost accepted a piece of toast from my hand, but shied away when Edith growled, and Mistake arrived with their food.

****

Veronica and her daughters were reunited with John Patrick when the war ended in 1945. They returned to Rochester Place in Kentish Town where they shared the Delaney family's Victorian terraced home with Veronica's aunts. Bin, Angela and Margaret shared the attic, Maureen had a small room on the top floor. Pattie, Veronica and John Patrick had rooms on the third floor and Veronica's aunt Kitty and aunt Rose had a small flat in the basement. Pattie was enrolled at St Mary's Abbey in Mill Hill, 4 kilometres down the road. She passed her 11-plus exams with distinction and was offered a place at Oxford University, but John Patrick couldn't afford the tuition fees. She applied for several scholarships and bursaries, but these were reserved for servicemen and women returning from the war and she was bitterly disappointed having to relinquish her seat at such a prestigious institution.

London had been badly damaged by the war, but the city finally had something to cheer about when it agreed to host the 1948 Summer Olympics, at short notice. Wembley Stadium had survived the bombings and was chosen as the main arena for the competition. Promotional posters were plastered on tree trunks and walls around the city. They pictured athletes housed in military barracks and school hostels but with food rationing still in place, competitors had to bring their own meals. That didn't matter: the Games would be the first televised major sporting event in history.

Britain hoped Maureen Gardener, Dorothy Manley, and Audrey Williamson would knock the flying housewife from Holland, Fanny Blankers-Koen, off her track and field perch. After all, how could the 30-year-old Dutch mother of two compete? Families lucky enough to own a television would be glued to it. Pattie knew then that she wanted to build a career in publicity and hoped to end up working in television.

She enrolled at the London School of Arts and studied Layout and Design and went on to Pitman's Secretarial College in Southampton Row. Her first job was as a junior designer for A & C Black Publishers in Soho Square, where she worked her way up to a position of "considerable" responsibility in the education department. Whenever she recalled this time of her life, Christianne and I always teased her about the type of work she did in Soho.

"Not that! Adam and Charles Black were esteemed publishers. They bought the copyright to publish Walter Scott's Waverley Novels, you know!" She protested.

It was during the 1948 Olympics in London that Pattie met my father, Ken. Aged 18, they were each other's first love, and had enough happiness to carry them through the hardships of post-war Britain. Their simple lives revolved around Sunday Mass and functions at St Dominic's Priory Social Club. Endless tandem cycle rides around Hampstead Heath and picnics in Rochester Square whiled away time saving for their wedding day and a honeymoon in Paris.

Shortly after completing his training as a telephone engineer, Ken received his two-year National Service notice and was despatched to West Berlin. The Soviet Union had blocked all rail, road and canal access to the area and the only way to get food to its two and half million residents was by air. Ken's unit of Royal Signals was tasked with keeping communications functional during the Berlin Airlift which saved the city from starvation. 270 000 flights landed with a total of two million tons of food.

As soon as his duty was done, he caught the fastest train home to marry his love, but a week before the wedding Pattie became unwell with terrible stomach pains. The doctor put it down to wedding nerves and the bells of St Dominic's Priory rang out in Camden Town in 1952. She collapsed on honeymoon seven days later with a burst appendix and flatlined in theatre. Her out-of-body experience was always a mystery, but she remembered watching the surgeons and nurses saving her life on the operating table below. Instead of a week of love-making and romantic strolls, Ken spent his honeymoon by his bride's hospital bed and took photographs of Paris at night, alone.

Pattie recuperated at the home of her French cousins in Le Donjon, south of Paris. She took the opportunity to brush up on her schoolgirl French and became a devoted fan of the singer Edith Piaf which caused us much suffering over the years to come. After her stay in France, she was rarely seen without a beret, or hat of some sort on her head.

She worked for A & C Black Publishers for five years and only resigned because she was pregnant with her first child Stephen. Her employer gave her a glowing reference describing her work ethic as "diligent, zesty, conscientious and hardworking". They concluded by saying that Pattie had a "pleasing personality", and they were sorry to see her go. Seventeen months after Stephen's birth, a second son, Mark, was born. Both pregnancies and births were difficult due to scarring from her earlier burst appendix operation. After Mark's birth most of her womb was removed and she thanked the Lord for the two beautiful boys that she had managed to have beforehand. Stephen and Mark were the first of the next-generation and they were doted on by aunts, uncles and grandparents who vied to babysit and take them on pram walks through the woodlands and meadows of Hampstead Heath. Their grandfather, John Patrick, was the first in line.

Pattie became a full-time mum and was content with her life until her sister Bin moved to Africa and letters from her started to arrive in the post. They described long sunny days, high teas, gin and tonics at elevenses, elephants and lions.

"Oh, Patrice, the houses and gardens are enormous. We have domestic staff to do the washing, gardening and ironing," Bin reported, underlining the last four words.

Bin had worked as a typist for Thomas Cook in Hampstead and had taken advantage of a staff-discounted cruise. Together with her best friend, Iris, they boarded the

Holland-Africa ship *Bloemfontein* to Cape Town, South Africa. On the return leg they moored in the port of Durban, and it was at a seafront bar that a handsome young farmer called Pieter tipped the head waiter £1.00 to be introduced to her. It was a lot of money at the time but worth every penny as it was love at first sight and when Bin arrived back in England, she announced that she was moving to Africa to marry her Southern Rhodesian farmer. Bin's courageous adventure lit a fire inside my mother and all her suppressed childhood thoughts and dreams once written into *Charles Letts's Schoolgirl Diary* came to the fore.

When the British Government launched a recruitment drive for young skilled Brits to relocate to Southern Rhodesia, Pattie and Ken jumped at the opportunity. In January 1958, their young family was vaccinated for cholera and yellow fever and boarded the HMV *Stirling Castle* to Cape Town. The journey took just over three weeks and was followed by a three-day train trip inland to the capital of Southern Rhodesia, Salisbury. They moved into immigrant flats in Mabelreign, and Ken started work with the Posts and Telecommunication Company. Once the boys were settled in a nursery school Pattie got a part-time job with Trifoil, an organisation that supported young immigrant Catholic families. Within the first month she contracted infectious hepatitis and for the second time in their short marriage, Ken nearly lost her again, but she recovered in time to attend Bin and Pieter's fabulous wedding in Odzi, east of Salisbury. Writing to her parents she described Bin's wedding outfit as a pale blue ballerina frock with a white hat trimmed with a pale blue veil. A beautiful spray of orchids decorated her handbag. Their eldest sister, Maureen arrived in Salisbury later that year and got a job with the Water Board before becoming a court stenographer, a job that she remained in for the rest of her life.

Shortly after Bin's wedding, a young South African engraver called Basil travelled to England to further his trade. Bin had met him during her visit to Cape Town and she insisted that he stayed with her parents in London. It didn't take long for his wonderful singing voice to swoop Veronica and John Patrick's fourth daughter, Angela, off her feet. They were married by Veronica's brother, who as parish priest of St Ives in Cornwall, made the occasion especially memorable. Basil returned to South Africa with his bride shortly after the wedding.

Three years later Ken accepted a transfer with the hydraulics department of the Posts and Telecommunications Company in Zomba. In 1961, the Beans packed up a tin trunk and caught a train 650 kilometres north to the British protectorate of Nyasaland, where Ken registered as an Overseas Civil Servant.

Nestled beneath the Zomba Plateau in the Shire Highlands of Southern Malawi they put down roots under a big blue African sky. Their three bedroomed home was modest with huge windows and large breezy rooms. An enormous veranda offered beautiful views of the garden and the surrounding landscape of Mexican Pine trees. Ken immediately bought a small second-hand boat and planned to take his boys fishing on Lake Chilwa at every opportunity. Pattie's letters to her parents embellished their life and John Patrick's imaginative replies described an old man joining them for elephant rides to picnic spots beneath acacia trees and swimming with hippos in the Shire River. Four out of his five children were now in Africa and over the next four years a further five grandchildren were born out there. He planned to visit them soon and was open to the possibility of moving to Africa permanently, but he never got the chance to visit. The family was devastated when he died suddenly of a heart attack.

After burying her husband in Camden, Veronica left England heartbroken with her youngest daughter Margaret. Margaret had recently qualified as a nurse, specialising in midwifery at Guy's Hospital in London and accepted a nursing post at Queen Elizabeth Hospital in Blantyre, Malawi. She accompanied her mother on a visit to see Angela in South Africa and Bin on the farm in Southern Rhodesia before joining Ken and Pattie in Malawi. Veronica left Malawi a year later and moved into a small flat with Maureen in Maxson Court in the centre of Salisbury.

By 1964 my mother's immediate family had all left England. Love and adventure brought them to Africa. I like the thought of that.

****

Wonder led me outside the perimeter fence to the enormous anthill that I'd noticed on our first walk to the lodge. To get a cell phone signal he said that I needed to crouch underneath the small acacia tree growing out the top of it. He kept watch for wild animals while I clambered into position but failed to get a connection. After my third attempt he rushed to my side and made an X in the soil on the exact spot, nudging me closer to his mark. Prickly acacia branches covered with spider webs wrapped their arms around me like a phone booth. It was a difficult pose for a difficult conversation.

Christianne wept in silent moments. No one had slept much since Pattie's arrival and the entire household had been on edge. Pattie had been distressed, kept calling my name and never stopped walking around the house. Whenever possible, Christianne's husband escaped from it all to the pub and their sons picked up on the strain and argued constantly. Scooby, their Alsatian-cross-husky, had been banished to the conservatory in case he knocked Pattie off her crutches; their hamster had been stopped from his daily whirls in an exercise ball to avoid a trip up. Locked external doors stopped Pattie wandering the roads, but caused Ziggy, their Jack Russell, to deposit steamy mounds on every carpet. The only creature getting any sleep was their dragon lizard, who had cleverly retreated into early hibernation under a small stone.

Christianne had been harshly reprimanded at work, her job was on the line, and she had little choice but to take Pattie to an Alzheimer's home that offered respite. Pattie was fine and the carers lovely, it sounded all too familiar. I hung onto the thought that this was only a temporary measure, but my promise to never put my mother in a home was broken and I totally understood why. I wrote down the contact number in the sand but couldn't bring myself to call, not right now! What would I say to her apart from I'm sorry which she couldn't understand anyway?

Wonder could tell that I'd had bad news and avoided eye contact out of respect. As I sat down at my desk a couple of elephants brushed against the perimeter fence, reaching for new leaves. They have incredible memories, if only Pattie had some of their genes. She couldn't remember her life and the only difference I could make right now was to write it down and remember it for her.

****

6

The Bean family settled into a tightly knit colonial society in the heart of Africa. Stephen and Mark were enrolled at Sir Harry Johnston British International School and Pattie got a temporary job as the Public Relations Officer for the Ministry of Information. Married women weren't allowed a permanent work contract and she wrote constantly to the Colonial Office at the injustice of it. Being a working mother was also sniffed at, but she couldn't have cared less.

Through her work, she met Derek and Gillian Bradfield, they became great friends and both families were rarely apart. The Bradfield's had five children who ganged up with Stephen and Mark for adventures exploring Wilson Falls or the potato market path for baboons and leopards. Racing their bikes down Mountain Road on the Zomba plateau was also a favourite pastime which left them with several childhood bodily scars. Ken taught them all how to fish and took them on many trips in his small boat. Lake Chilwa was the closest fishing spot to home, but it was often affected by seasonal rains and summer evaporation. They tried their luck at trout farms in the area and occasionally went further afield to Lake Malawi, bringing home delicious Chambo freshwater bream for dinner.

Derek and Gillian persuaded Pattie and Ken to join the Zomba Theatre Group which operated out of the Gymkhana club. They were swooped up into a vibrant community of amateur theatrics and rapidly got involved in a variety of productions. Ken was the stage manager while Pattie contributed to the choreography in *Cinderella*. She was the prompt in *Next Time I'll Sing to You* and slipped into a skimpy bikini top and pantaloons for an Egyptian snake dance in *The Salad Days* where Ken acted as PC Boot. He sang *"Daisy, Daisy"* with Gillian and managed a professional version of the sand dance with Derek in a series of acts called *A Victorian Evening*.

Ken was renowned for his sense of humour and became a popular member of Zomba Country Club where he was an avid golfer. Cramming another golfing trophy onto the mantelpiece, Pattie declared that she was becoming a golfing widow, but kept busy playing squash on Saturdays and running weekly keep fit classes for mums. She went to church every Sunday and developed lifelong friendships with John and Pat Deary, Cynthia and Paddy McGee, Betty Collins, Kay Pearson, Helen Bannister and Jean Kay.

In 1964, His Royal Highness, Prince Philip, saluted the Union Jack as it was lowered at the national sports stadium in Blantyre. British rule in Nyasaland came to an end and the country's name changed to Malawi under the leadership of Doctor Hastings Kamuzu Banda. It was a busy time for Pattie's public relations role as the new Malawian Government set about showing the world that they could govern just as well as the British.

One of her first tasks was to design a commemorative plaque for His Imperial Majesty, Emperor Haile Selassie's three-day visit. *The Lion of Judah* as he was known, was the first head of state to pay an official visit to independent Malawi. The man of many titles jetted into Chileka Airport and was met by Doctor Banda and an army parade. The streets were lined with bunting and crowded with people waving the newly adopted Malawian flag. During the visit, Selassie accorded members of the new Malawian Government several incredible honours. Dr Banda received the *Collar of*

The Order of the Queen of Sheba, the Governor General received the honour of *Grand Cordon of the Order of Trinity*, and the Commissioner of Police was made a *Commander of the Order of Menelik II*, to name just a few. In return Banda named a street in Blantyre after Selassie and gave him the title of *Great King of Malawi*. Selassie unveiled Pattie's small plaque at a ceremony on Zomba Plateau, overlooking the Mulanje Mountains. She found it hard going trying to remember all their titles and felt they were all completely upstaged by Selassie's diminutive pet Chihuahua, called Lulu!

Banda was brought up by a single parent, his mother. Initially, he pushed for the empowerment of women which Pattie greatly admired but he refused to introduce television into the country. His belief that it would somehow pollute Malawian culture meant that Pattie's dream of working in the industry would have to wait.

When she was seconded to the Extension Aids office of the Ministry of Agriculture, her life became the adventure she had longed for. On a salary of £53.80 a month and bursting with new design ideas from Soho, she produced 25 000 copies of the monthly magazine *Farm News*. She designed posters on how to cycle safely on the newly tarred roads, placing them strategically on fruit trees where villagers gathered to pick food. Perhaps Charles Letts's diary had influenced the design - "*do not ride with feet on handlebars or without hands!*"

Put in charge of an audio-visual production unit, she created a mobile puppet theatre out of papier-mâché. Its main character was a teacher named Bambo Jomba and together with her assistant, Oliver Kayamba Phiri, they travelled to rural schools and villages presenting plays from the back of a Land Rover. Crowds gathered out of curiosity and listened to lessons on conservation and best farming practices blasting out from two enormous loudspeakers attached to the roof rack. The flamboyant puppet spoke in the local language of

Chichewa and his teachings were reinforced by a flood of brochures and posters left behind in the Land Rover's dust for everyone to study.

The puppet theatre crossed rivers on wooden rafts, travelled down bush paths and climbed hills to get their message across to the widest possible audience. Pattie fell in love with the gentleness of the Malawian people and often found herself seated on grass mats as the guest of honour at weddings in the middle of nowhere. Witnessing families becoming more self-sufficient with their improved harvests cemented her belief that education changed lives.

Bambo Jomba became a local celebrity. The educational effectiveness of his plays was noticed by other government departments who started to allocate budgets for similar presentations. Pattie was soon working full time, despite the social norms.

Banda founded the state-run Malawi Broadcasting Corporation and distributed free government radios throughout the country to communicate with his people. Pattie's mobile puppet theatre was launched into communities with instructions on how they worked. She was returning home after a particularly bumpy trip when she developed terrible stomach pains and Ken rushed her to the doctor. Most of her womb had been removed ten years ago so she knew that she couldn't be pregnant and suspected some sort of blockage. Two weeks later she got the news and telephoned her mother in Salisbury.

"Mary Mother of God! I thought you couldn't have any more children. Your eldest is 11 years old!" Veronica shrieked with excitement.

"I know mommy, it's a miracle!" Pattie squealed.

Ken and Pattie had regretfully accepted years ago that they couldn't have any more children. The shock of having a new baby together with memories of broken nights, teething and tight budgets created a lot of uncertainty. Pattie poured several large cups of tea while Ken poured something a lot stronger; the misgivings of their changing situation hitting him particularly hard. The baby could only grow to the size of what little womb Pattie had left and was unlikely to survive but once she got through the first trimester, she dared to dream about having a little girl.

Around the same time, Pattie also received an education grant for Stephen and Mark to attend St Michael's boarding school in Salisbury. It was one of the best private schools in Africa, 650 kilometres away in Rhodesia. With a new school and a new sibling on its way, Stephen and Mark's lives were flipped upside down as well.

To allay their fears, Pattie piled on the positives hoping to turn it into a wonderful adventure for them. She described exciting journeys to school by road and rail, weekends at Bin's farm driving tractors and learning to shoot. When they were back from boarding school, they could teach the new baby to swim, cycle and fish. Pattie's excitement soon spread and with Ken's help, the boys built a fort from old parquet flooring in preparation for playtime with their new sibling. Stephen and Mark drew up a list of potential names, 25 for boys and 2 for girls. The family dynamic was about to change but they would all manage, somehow.

Having grown just three centimetres in girth in five months, Pattie was able to hide her pregnancy from work colleagues. Pregnant women were not supposed to work, and she enjoyed the deceit of what she thought was a very chauvinistic rule. She could also sense that her work environment was changing and detected a slight disdain developing towards anyone connected to a colonial past. Bambo Jomba's scripts were severely edited and started to carry forms of propaganda. The free radios were also broadcasting a more sinister message. She took pride in being apolitical and with a heavy heart, handed Bambo Jomba over to a new more obliging team.

She turned her energy towards adult literacy and equality, which included teaching imprisoned women and children. It was at the prisons that she discovered a basic philosophy which greatly appealed: "The African village lives for the day and lives each day to the full, with no great expectation for the morrow".

Stephen and Mark had just got home from boarding school for the Christmas holidays when Pattie went into labour and was rushed to Zomba Hospital. When it became clear that she needed an emergency caesarean, they sent her by ambulance to Queen Elizabeth Hospital, 65 kilometres away in Blantyre. A baby girl was born three months premature, weighing a meagre 1.3 kilogrammes and just 23 centimetres long. At a rushed provisional baptism in the hospital, Pattie and Ken named her Christianne Mary Veronica, which sounded suspiciously like the Stations of the Cross! It was touch and go whether their baby would survive but Pattie's sister Margaret was Sister in Charge of the maternity ward and was determined not to lose a niece on her watch.

Pattie asked to be discharged early so she could spend the last few days with her boys before they returned to boarding school. Christianne remained behind in an incubator for seven weeks under Margaret's watchful eye. With help from the Zomba Police and permission from the British High Commissioner, Pattie arranged for her expressed breast milk to be sent to the hospital every day. A policeman left Zomba for Blantyre each morning with a diplomatic bag strapped to one hand and a cold bag of bottled breast milk in the other. Knowing the contents, he blushed each time he took delivery and Pattie made it clear which parcel was more precious, quite sure that Her Majesty would understand.

Christianne quickly became the focus of the entire family.

She was so small and wrinkly that Ken joked she had the appearance of a cobbled army sock but apart from a few difficulties with her ears, she was perfectly formed and the absolute apple of his eye.

It was not long after her birth that Banda's dictatorial intentions became obvious. He consolidated his power and declared Malawi a single-party state under the Malawi Congress Party. Every adult citizen had to be a member of the Party and was forced to carry the card. Spot checks were regularly conducted by the police. State-issued photographs of Banda had to be hung in every office and home and a law was passed preventing anything from being placed higher than it. It became an offence to publish anything that may undermine government authority which was punishable by 5 years imprisonment. New conservative policies banned women from wearing trousers or showing cleavage. Men with long hair had to have it cut at the airport before entering the country. Citizens were locked out of their houses and forced to attend rallies. Vacancies and promotions were given to indigenous Malawians, who were frantically trained up as successors to colonial posts. Government departments were hit first, and British civil servants started to emigrate by their thousands. Pattie's hero had become a villain.

While they were debating whether to remain in Malawi or not, another miracle occurred. 15 months after Christianne was born, I came into the world, also three months premature and weighing marginally heavier at 1.6 kilograms. Margaret again managed the difficulties of a premature niece and popped me into a glass box with a light bulb for warmth.

"Just like a chicken," she giggled.

Ever grateful for the carriage of her breast milk to Blantyre, Pattie named me after the reigning British Monarch. Rather than spelling my name with a 'z' she felt the letter 's' made Elisabeth sound softer. Names of a couple of good friends from Zomba Club were added, as well as Pattie's maiden name for prosperity. Five names in total that would make it impossible for me to insert my full identity onto any application form in the future. I was only 28 centimetres long; my name on the birth certificate looked longer!

Despite having two babies, Pattie continued voluntary work in the prisons and remained involved with the Zomba Theatre Club, helping with costume design, and arranging the dances in the production of *Toad of Toad Hall*. But when Ken lost his job to indigenisation, both were unemployed and had few prospects left in Malawi. Ken returned to England to find work and planned to send funds while Pattie remained behind for the boys to finish the school year. Africa had brought our family together and we were about to be torn apart.

To cut costs, she moved into Christianne's godmother's house, on her tea estate in Zomba and to make ends meet, she developed a fashion line of hand-painted batik dresses. In 1968, the dresses won first prize at the Fashion Crafts and Fabric Show, first prize at the Independence Trade Fair and the Lilongwe Agricultural Show but they never brought in enough money. Ken's contribution was even less and after six months of struggling, she'd had enough. Margaret helped load our old Mercedes with the tin trunk and drove with Pattie and her babies to Rhodesia and our family left Malawi for good. Fellow puppeteer, Oliver Kayamba Phiri, wrote in his farewell message:

"Mrs Bean, you cannot imagine how hard it is for us to really express how much we are going to miss you. The sweet memories of your stay with us here in Malawi, and particularly the Extension Aids branch, will long be treasured in our hearts. You have really shown us nothing can be achieved without co-operation and for this we really give our thanks. Remember us when you reach home as we shall in your absence. If God permits, we hope to meet you again."

****

I excused myself from afternoon fishing and left the dinner table early. Lying under the mosquito net stories of another beautiful day in the Ume drifted upstairs, but a broken promise and dreadful images of my mother in the respite home, made for a restless night.

****

7

The call of the fish eagle woke me to another magical morning in the Ume. That, and an annoying sweeping sound coming from the swimming pool area outside. After another battle with the mosquito net, I stomped over to the balcony and scowled into the sunlight searching for the perpetrator. Great white egrets were pecking at the lawn and hippos splashed in the shallows of the river guarding a young calf. A troop of vervet monkeys rustled in the fronds having been chased to the palm tops by Mistake and his grass broom! His vigorous brush strokes on the glitterstone tiles were keeping the monkeys from raiding the breakfast table and was the source of the irritating sound that had woken me up. The monkeys chattered nervously when Mistake waved good morning to me and used his broom to point them out. I returned a weak wave and marched downstairs in a mood after a bad night.

The smell of mince and toast filled the lounge, which Edith had already sniffed out and demanded her share before I sat down. Gertrude almost took a slice from me but pranced away like a drum majorette when a snake moved in the thatch near my desk. Leaning in for a better look, I could see yellow stripes on its long pale brown body which turned in my direction just as Edith bleated for more treats and gave me a fright.

"Stop it Edith, there's a snake!" I yelled.

Hearing the word snake, Mistake bounded towards me, wild eyed, swirling the broom over his head and shouting out what I knew to be the Shona word for snake.

"Nyoka! Nyoka!"

Edith fled to the bottom of the garden, monkeys sprang from the palm tops over the fence and into the bush. Every bird took flight, shrieking alarm calls. With all the commotion I suddenly felt vulnerable and leapt off the veranda arming myself with the pool leaf scoop shouting, "Mistake, Mistake, there's a snake!" which sounded odd.

Mistake skidded to a stop at my desk with his broom in spear mode. He gave the creature a nudge with the handle, and it recoiled into a hole in the thatch.

"Eish, it's a Tsanga Nyoka," he said, walking off with no further explanation.

Reassured by his nonchalance, I continued to write but struggled to concentrate when every dried leaf hissed on the floor, palm fronds grew fangs and arum lilies pulled forked tongues! When Tsanga Nyoka did reappear, it gave me a good look before slithering down the thatch and across the patio towards the lounge suite. Re-armed with the leaf scoop, I tried to guide it into the net, pushing the couches aside each time it went for cover underneath. It got annoyed with my rescue efforts and latched onto the scoop which I let fly across the room. The net broke off the pole and hit the thatch, showering me with bits of straw and Tsanga Nyoka took the opportunity to slither back across the patio, up the thatch and back into its hole.

Curious about the noise, Wonder appeared from his kitchen. Speaking in Tonga, he got a full update on events from Mistake before gathering the remains of the leaf scoop.

"It's a Tsanga Nyoka," he advised.

I already knew that but before I damaged anything else, he quickly added that it was a snake that caused "little pain" and that I should just ignore it. After considering what that pain threshold might be, I dragged my desk to the maximum stretch of the electricity cord and put my feet up on a wooden stool for good measure.

In its final appearance, Tsanga Nyoka popped out from its hole, looked left and right for the leaf scoop before making a dash for the tall grass beyond the fence, just before the rumble of Hans' motorbike announced that it was fishing time again.

We followed Mistake and the cooler box, to the bottom of the garden. Edith and her family fell into line behind us and were diverted by a scattering of cheese crackers from Jules.

"It's not for you Edith," we all said in unison.

After a couple of days in the Ume, the slightly bizarre seemed perfectly normal and Mistake pushed the boat off into the water with his usual shout of "tight lines!"

If we wanted the best chance of catching a decent sized tiger fish, we needed to go back to Bird Island. I was not enthralled about spending the morning with hippos, but Hans had many fishing trophies to his name and at one point held the Ultra-Light world record for catching an 8.7kg tiger fish on a 2kg line! With his reassurance and thoughts of a catching a similar size, I succumbed but swivelled my seat in the opposite direction, so I didn't have to watch the boat dodging the grumpy pod.

Our last visit to Bird Island was too brief to appreciate that it was thick with trees and shrubs and shook with birdlife when Hans tied the boat up to a leaning branch. Once the engine was turned off, cattle egrets swooped back into their nests on the top branches, forming a layer of white icing on the green tree canopy. Darters zoomed in to their hungry chicks in the middle layer and brown finches fluttered along a thin pebble beach unperturbed with the waves created by the wallowing hippos.

Hans could see that I was distracted by the hippos and gave detailed instructions on the fishing tackle as a diversion. We checked the trace knot, split-shot weights, sharpness of the hook, line strength and drag tension. Bushy was given the first sliver of bream fillet that had been frozen from yesterday's catch and a slice was then woven onto each of our lethal-looking fishing hooks.

"Presentation is everything," Hans advised.

With one eye on the hippos, my first cast was manic.

"Toss the line out smoothly for better distance and reel in with rhythm," Hans added.

My second attempt was better, and I eventually relaxed and got into a rhythm, casting out and reeling in again and again. It became hypnotic and my mind started to drift when an enormous dragonfly landed on the tip of my rod. I wondered how it coped with the Kariba winds and how its delicate wings weren't ripped to shreds. Did the darters living in the middle layer of Bird Island live in constant fear of being pooped on by the cattle egrets above them or were the egrets considerate enough to shuffle to one side before letting one go? What was the purpose of life of the sticky moth fluttering around Jules as she studied the darter chicks in their nests?

"Hans, is it the bird droppings that attract the tiger fish to the island?" I asked innocently, throwing out another cast.

"Partly. The tiger fish are also here for the chicks that fall out of their nests," he replied.

Jules immediately went onto lifeguard duty, casting her line where she could keep a watchful eye out for the chicks. Suddenly her reel screamed, and Bushy leapt out from under the console barking for another fish sliver. Bird Island emptied with all the noise and Hans roared at me to wind in my line to give Jules uncluttered waters.

Jules ran from side to side following her line, fighting her fish and creating waves which rocked the boat into the island. Disturbed by the raucous, the hippos turned to face us, and one dived in our direction. I wanted to bring to everyone's attention, but the tiger fish took priority and after a 5-minute battle Jules brought a whopper on board. We didn't have a scale, but Hans estimated that it was four kilograms plus and after a few quick photographs, he released it gently back into the water. Whatever the weight, it was the biggest fish Jules had ever caught. While she celebrated with a bitterly cold beer, Hans instructed me to cast out in the same place where Jules had just had success. It was very close to where the hippo had just disappeared underwater, and I hoped that I wouldn't hook onto it. Had anyone ever brought in a hippo on a tiger fish line?

As the split-shot weight on my line hit the water my rod arched, and the reel screamed.

"Yes!" Hans shouted, bringing Bushy out from under the console again.

The hippo surfaced at the same time, blowing out water angrily from its nostrils but it was far enough away from my line to know that it wasn't attached to it. Egrets and darters circled the island deciding whether it was safe to return and while Jules scanned the waves for any bobbing chicks, my silvery tiger fish leapt out the water into the air.

"Hans, I've got one!" I squealed.

"Keep the tip of your rod up; don't let your line go slack," he instructed. "Play it, play it – now reel!"

As the fish got closer to the boat, it took everything I had not to jump in and grab it by hand, hippos and all, but it made another swim for freedom, pulling more line from my reel.

"Keep your tip up," Hans repeated, above Bushy's bark.

My hands cramped and the rod handle pinched into my belly button which Hans didn't care about, although we all paused for a second when something plopped down from a branch; fortunately, it was a wild fig and not a baby darter.

"That's it, wind in and keep your tit up!" Hans shouted

desperately.

"My tit?" I shrieked.

"No man, your tip!" He replied embarrassed.

"That's up too!" I squealed.

After an eternity of tip and tits upping and belly button ripping, my fish eventually tired. I guided it onto its side at the edge of the boat and Hans scooped it into the landing net with a teacher's smile. Finally, I was a tiger fisherwoman with a four-point-something kilogram beauty to my name. Photographs were taken quickly in every position before releasing it back into the water. The boat bubbled with joy; even more so because Hans let me drive it back home.

"A complete fisherwoman must know how to drive a boat," Hans said.

Each second of our fabulous catch was retold on a booze cruise back to the lodge. I ignored the hippos, breezed through the pod, revved the engine, and beached the boat onto shore like a master. Mistake and Wonder were disappointed by the empty keep net but clapped when Jules showed them the photographs of our magnificent tiger fish.

"It would have been a good fish to smoke and eat," Wonder commented on our waste of food.

The family joined us for dinner and tiger fish revelry. Details of our fabulous catch became more and more exaggerated as the evening progressed. I pranced around the room a few times, cupping my breasts, reassuring Hans of their upright position! The girls whispered more plans for the surprise fiftieth birthday celebration tomorrow night and from their excitement, Debbie deduced that a party had been planned and disliked the fuss. For some reason, life felt less cruel, I would get hold of the respite home tomorrow, no matter what!

****

8

I slept in for the first time and missed my morning ritual with Edith and Gertrude who were already dozing under the fig tree by the time I came downstairs. It was a scorcher of a day and through an ancient set of binoculars I counted 37 elephants on the Matusadona shoreline. Some were enjoying a mud bath at the edge of the water while the rest of the herd grazed the savanna on the foreshore. I zoomed in on their dexterous trunks gently pulling up tufts of grass, beating the roots to rid them of soil before scooping the bundles into their V-shaped mouths. With a burst of testosterone, a cheeky young bull galumphed down the bank with its ears flapping trumpeting its charge towards a cattle egret innocuously pecking for insects in the mud. When the small bird saw what was coming it opened its wings and chased the young bull all the way back to its mother!

Today was Debbie's birthday and Wonder had made a light breakfast of French toast to see us through the day before the dinner party. After layering a few slices with Marmite, I sat down at my desk and Edith was in front of me in a flash. Her nostrils flared when the Marmite stuck to her gums, but it didn't bother Gertrude who appeared from nowhere and snatched half a slice from my hand at last!

The girls had arranged to take Debbie to Tiger Bay for the morning, clearing the way for Jules and me to decorate the dining room and for Wonder to prepare the surprise banquet. He came up behind me to collect my plate and to confirm the number of potatoes to cook for the dinner party.

"How's your book?" he asked.

"Coming along, I'm on chapter 8," I smiled. "Are you able to take me back to the anthill before you start cooking, I need to speak to my mother?"

I found the X mark in the sand easily and got through to the respite home on my first attempt, but the connection was lousy, and I had to shout an introduction to the manager.

"Hold on a minute, love, I need to find her for you," he yelled down the phone.

"It's your daughter from Zimbabwe," I heard him saying as he handed the phone over to Pattie.

"What?" She said, grabbing the handset before going mute.

"Hello! Hello! Mum, are you there? It's me, Lissie. How are you?" I said, upbeat.

"Oh, hello Darling, how are the animals?"

A full sentence! Could the home be the right place for her? Her voice sounded sluggish, but so good to hear.

"They are fine. Scruffy has had his summer grooming; Muffin still chases her toys everywhere," I replied, surveying the Jesse bush for the buffalo bull.

"I loved you for so long. When are you coming, darling?" Another full sentence!

"I love you too, Mum. I'll come soon," I answered, guilt ridden.

I wanted to ask normal questions about her room and whether she had made any friends but knew she couldn't respond so I rambled on about the Ume River and Edith instead.

"You'd love her, Mum. She's a strong woman."

"Sorry love, she's gone," the manager interrupted.

Pattie had handed the phone back to him without another word to me. He explained that she had settled in well, but they faced a constant battle to get her to rest her crippled legs. She paced the corridors on her crutches, but a new sedative should help slow her down.

I pressed the red button on my mobile and held back my tears all the way to the lodge, caring less if buffaloes trampled me to death. We still had a few hours before the decorations needed to be hung so I retreated upstairs to be alone with my laptop and another wad of tissues.

****

When we arrived in Salisbury, Rhodesia in 1969, the country had troubles. It had been a self-ruled British territory for 42 years and wanted independence like the rest of the colonies. Britain refused to grant it because a prerequisite to decolonisation was that there must be majority rule. Ian Smith's white minority government rejected this and, in 1965, had declared Rhodesia unilaterally independent from Britain (UDI). The United Nations considered the act illegal and imposed sanctions. Rhodesia was unrecognised and isolated from most countries of the world, and, because its government refused to hand over power to the black majority, a guerrilla war gathered momentum under the leadership of Robert Mugabe and Joshua Nkomo, but that was out in the bush and not in the towns. Yet.

Pattie's immediate priority was to get work and put a roof over our heads. While Margaret babysat Christianne and me in a hotel room, Pattie went for job interviews and quickly accepted a position with Lindsay Smithers Advertising Agency. On a salary of $100 per month, she rented a small house in Mabelreign and filled it with furniture borrowed from family or donated from members of Our Lady of the Wayside church in Mount Pleasant. Christianne and I were so small that she used orange fruit crates as cribs which she felt worked perfectly well. Stephen and Mark remained at boarding school but when Margaret returned to Malawi, Pattie had no choice but to put Christianne and me in day care. I was just under three years old at the time.

When Ken suddenly returned from England our family dynamic changed again. He found work as a draftsman for the local municipality and with two incomes, my parents could afford to get a mortgage on a four-bedroomed home on Quorn Avenue, close to Pattie's church.

The property had an enormous swimming pool and a garden of Jacaranda trees with rope swings that offered hours and hours of simple fun. Jasmine and honeysuckle hedges snaked around the boundary fence and made Pattie sneeze each morning like clockwork. They were so pretty and fragrant that she refused to chop them out, despite her hay fever. Ken built us a fort in a sturdy loquat tree in the back garden and to complete our family, we adopted two rescue dogs and a cat from the SPCA. Twinks the tabby cat ruled the house and Kelly the Rhodesian ridgeback guarded the perimeter fence. A cheeky Maltese poodle ruled over Pattie who she gave the fantastic name of Ringo Star and loved that it drew stares when she called out his name. Ringo became her chief bodyguard and didn't seem to mind that he was a constant shade of pink after visits to the parlour. He barked a lot of the time, but especially when Pattie told him how beautiful he looked.

The Lemon family lived next door, Mrs Bean and Mrs Lemon continuously mocked each other about their surnames. They looked forward to having Mrs Sprout or Mrs Plum move into the neighbourhood. Pattie felt that their fruit and veg names would make it easier for friends and family to find us in our new home. The house was always full of friends from church or visitors from Malawi and the swimming pool was a wash of red Speedo school costumes worn by Stephen, Mark, and fellow boarders staying over on weekends. Having left Malawi, Margaret and her fiancé Christopher came to stay with us for a while as they searched for a new home. Margaret was pleased to see that although we were small, her nieces were developing at a steady rate. Pattie put our healthy growth pattern down to the fact that she had joined the Positive Health Association where she met Tilly and Neil Jackson who became lifelong friends. Their children Robbie and Laurie frequently stayed the night while Tilly and Pattie concocted the next healthy recipe. Their meals were usually very green in colour, providing an overload of minerals and vitamins that we required.

Christianne started school at the Dominican Convent and was the youngest and smallest in her class. Her uniforms were all too big for her, but Pattie felt that they gave her lots of room to grow. She left for school wearing a light blue tunic which fell below her knees. If Pattie took the hem up any further the garment would look like a lamp shade. Her baggy beige blazer had to have the sleeves rolled up and a huge pudding basin hat sat just below her nose. She met her lifelong friend, Annie, on the first day but her first year at school was hampered by problems with her ears. She had several operations which included the fitting of grommets to prevent the accumulation of fluid and infection in the middle ear.

I joined them both at the Convent a year later and met my first school friend, Laura, in the swimming team. We did everything together and it was not unusual to see us skateboarding or playing an unladylike game of marbles on the school green at break time. While I got to grips with learning to spell my own enormously long name, the names of teachers like Sr. Pancratius, Sr. Veneranda, Sr. Octavia and Sr. Gratiana proved equally as challenging, and I tended to lean towards those I could pronounce and spell like Sr. Therese, Sr. Catherine, Sr. Vincent and Mrs Armitage.

Annie and Laura frequently spent the night and joined the furore in our new home which was often so full that we slept on cushions or mattresses on the floor.

Ken sold our old Mercedes and replaced it with a roomier VW Kombi which he used to drive us to the beaches of Beira in Mozambique for most school holidays. The Kombi had been converted to carry a fridge, stove, a set of bunk beds and a fold away card table that made travelling an enormous amount of fun for his four children, with cheap accommodation by the sea.

He left his job with the municipality and built up a good reputation as a freelance draftsman and was successful for a while. It was the only time in my childhood that I remember him being around for any period but as the bush war intensified, he found it harder to get work and it wasn't long before it dried up completely. While he developed an interest in the totes at Borrowdale racecourse, Pattie joined one of the largest advertising agencies in the country, Mathewman, Banks and Tholet. She was made an account executive and with it came the opportunity to work in film and television, at last! Her creative flare didn't go unnoticed when she pumped Chanel No 5 perfume through the air conditioning at the launch of the SA Tours film on Flowers of South Africa, and her name appeared in the newspapers with good reviews.

When Ken suffered a heart attack driving back from the horse races, the crash of his car into the ditch outside our gate signalled change again. He developed the shakes, putting an end to any draftsman's work, and he took solace in the arms of someone else. Heartbroken and left with a mortgage, school and legal fees, Pattie put our home on the market. Stephen and Mark left for England to further their studies and Ringo Star was suddenly the only man left in our lives. It was a role he took very seriously.

During the period of my parents' separation, Pattie

combined a business trip to England with a 10-day shoestring camping adventure around Europe. The excitement of going on an aeroplane for the first time, visiting our brothers, and living in a tent, deflected the ordeal of Ken moving out and our homelessness. Pattie met quietly with his family in London to explain that despite her very Catholic beliefs, divorce was inevitable.

My brother Stephen and his friend Sean Bradfield from Malawi joined us on the camping trip. They drove us through Germany, Switzerland, Belgium, Holland, and France. We pitched our tent near the Heidelberg Castle, Herman the German, and in the Black Forest. The railway journey up to the Jungfrau Mountain fulfilled Pattie's lifelong desire to visit the Alps. We saw snow for the first time and lived on large cups of tea and huge chunks of French bread with cheese. As children, we couldn't have been more excited, nor more shielded from the outcome of a looming divorce.

On our return to Salisbury, Pattie signed up with a house-sitting agency and we moved from house to house until she could afford to rent a cottage in Chancing Lane in Borrowdale. Christianne and I shared the upstairs loft and fought constantly over dividing lines in the room. Our contrasting personalities and interests led to a healthy sibling rivalry. A particularly contentious issue was whether my picture of Red Rum encroached on Christianne's picture of David Cassidy!

We didn't have much but we were happy, and if Pattie had any worries, she hid them away from us in the seclusion of her box bedroom downstairs. The only time Christianne and I felt vulnerable was when Pattie went to hospital for a hip replacement. It was considered a big operation at the time and having a large chunk of steel inserted into our mother's leg was a terrifying thought.

"It's from an old sports injury, I was Games Captain at St

Mary's Abbey you know!" she reiterated.

She was in traction for a week with metal staples running from her hip down to her knee. We had never seen our mother looking so ill and thought she was going to die. Hearing her cry in pain at all hours of the night we took her mug after mug of tea to try and "fix everything," like she said it would. She would squeeze us into her bed, wrap her arms around us and sing us to sleep with '*The Mountains of Mourn,*' '*Mighty like a Rose*' or '*We Ain't Got a Barrel of Money*', while she prayed for our ship to come in.

Pattie never spoke badly about Ken and wrote in her Christmas newsletter that year that she was grateful for the 25 years of real happiness with him. I saw my father twice after the divorce. On the first visit, he handed me the only page of his book, *Ivory Black*, which was typed on a manual typewriter from his bedsit. He described himself as a non-conformist in politics and religion. This, and his favourite CD of the *Best of Roger Whitaker*, was at that time, the most I really knew about him. On our last visit he used up a box of Polaroid film on Christianne and me. Seven years later he collapsed in sheltered housing and died at Lewisham Hospital in England. When Pattie heard the news, she pulled the car over, fell onto the bonnet and sobbed, which I didn't understand at the time.

****

9

Balloons bobbed in the wind and an enormous fiftieth birthday banner reflected in the lounge mirror. I pinned fairy lights from one corner of the lounge to the other while Jules put the finishing touches on a large handmade birthday card by sticking dried grasses and a guinea fowl feather on the front. She placed it on the dining room table next to Wonder's display of arum lilies and swan-shaped serviettes, for all to see.

Debbie was delighted with the effort we'd made and thoroughly embarrassed by our rowdy rendition of happy birthday, which included the use of saucepans as drums. Wonder received a loud cheer, when he walked in wearing an oversized chef's hat for the occasion. It was so tall that it almost clipped the ceiling fan when he presented buttered asparagus starters. Favourite tunes of Engelbert Humperdinck played in the background and enormous quantities of gem squash, carrots and roast potatoes were placed on the table. Paula rocked Jordan to sleep in his pram and pots of gravy steamed next to chilled bottles of wine. *Sweet Caroline* was in full swing when Wonder returned from the kitchen with an enormous leg of roast lamb and all conversation stopped.

Hans assured us it was not related to Edith, but Jules ate only the vegetables just in case and promised to do a roll call in the morning. Any further conversation on the matter was carefully avoided for the rest of the meal and we had a beautiful, memorable evening in the African bush. Dancing and more banging of saucepans carried on late into the night.

Debbie's children and their families left for Harare early the next morning. It was always a sad goodbye and Jules invited her over for lunch to cheer her up and to spend our last day in the Ume chilling by the pool. Debbie had established that Chuck had extended his stay and wouldn't be on our boat transfer, which was a shame, I'd hoped to apologise for my earlier rudeness. We'd only seen him once when Hans took us on a tour of the crocodile farm, but he kept his distance.

Hans popped in to say goodbye and chatted about his day's work making improvements at the junior school in the employees' compound. Debbie added that the two fabulous teachers, Mike and Witness were struggling with classes as they were one teacher short. It was a shame as the children were adorable and so eager to learn. I could tell by the silence this had piqued Jules' interest.

"You'd need to learn the Tonga language," I chipped in, but it was an interesting possibility.

Our final sundowners on the veranda were subdued. We were miserable at the thought of leaving but not sure how safe we'd feel in the lodge without Adam and Charn. We started packing in daylight in case we felt scared, and Wonder looked downcast stuffing the tin trunk with our fishing equipment and the last of the groceries from the pantry. Mistake was thoroughly miserable piling it all up by the back door, ready for the wheelbarrow run to the harbour at first light.

We were in bed by the time the sun disappeared behind the Matusadona mountains. Tucked under the mosquito we felt safe and surprisingly at ease listening to the lions roaring and hyenas cackling in the distance. The waning crescent moon made for a dark night and all sorts of unusual insects were attracted to our headlamps that we were using to read and write. A few armoured-plated varieties bounced against the net trying to get in and nightjars and bats swooped in on the hunt, their familiarity was oddly comforting.

In the quiet of the night, we could hear hippos eating grass on land again. Strangely enough, I would miss them too. Their munching noises carried through the air and sounded much closer to the lodge than usual. Out of curiosity I got out of bed to have a look, but the light from my headlamp was too weak to see anything from the balcony. In a moment of madness, I suggested to Jules that we go outside and investigate.

Following the narrow beams of light on our foreheads we tiptoed downstairs and across the veranda. After dodging every crispy leaf on the lawn, we stopped behind an inadequately sized mopane tree near the fence. The hippos were so close we could smell them which Jules confirmed with a jab into my ribs and gave me fright. Just a single mesh fence separated us from the world's fourth largest mammal, and we started to giggle. By the time a zillion sticky moths swarmed our headlamps, we were buckled over laughing in silence, trying not to pee in our brooks, until a hippo snorted, and we froze with fear.

Peeping out from either side of the tree trunk we came face to face with a hippopotamus calf with soft spots that were still pink with newness. Its colossal mother blended ominously into the night and was using her massive head to push her baby closer to the green lawn growing through the fence, centimetres away from us!

"They are right here!" I mimed, moulded to the tree.

We watched in awe, barely breathing until the wind changed direction and blew zillions of sticky moths away from our headlamps. Mama hippo lifted her head, sniffed out the potential danger from two, three-eyed buffoons hiding behind a tree and reared. Her snort shook the ground, and, from the inner depths of absolute fear, I let out a guttural roar, "Ruunn!" Adrenaline carried us across the lawn like the wind, hurdling the veranda steps into the lodge, leaping onto the stairway taking two steps at a time with Jules pushing from behind, until the bedroom door was bolted, and we were back under the mosquito net, heaving for breath, laughing with fright. Curious about the outcome I sprang out of bed again expecting to see a pod of angry hippos tearing up the front garden, but they had fled in the opposite direction to the safety of the water.

Jules teased me about my Edith-like growl, saying she'd never heard anything quite like it! Neither had I! After a few exaggerated demonstrations I collapsed on the bed and burst into an uncontrollable, belly-wobbling laugh. Writing my mother's story was somehow healing my heart and I wanted more of it. In a deep growl I suggested we extend our stay in the Ume by a few more days. The excess groceries would do for meals, and we could always go fishing. Jules was on annual leave: I had a painting contract starting only in a week and Hildah had our home and animals sorted. Our only dilemma was that Jules' medicine would run out. If we could find a way of getting it to the Ume in a day or so, we'd stay longer. I turned on my laptop and gave it a rub, willing it to give me more time.

****

10

Pattie replaced Ken's VW Kombi with a more practical two-door, 1961 Morris Minor. Its green exterior was polished with turtle wax and hid a souped-up engine with devilish twin 1000 SU carburettors. Mag wheels, a racing steering wheel and a loud pink Maltese poodle straddling the dashboard, added to its charm.

When Pattie collected us from school, her approach was easily tracked by the noise from Ringo's barking and the rumble of the Morris engine at every traffic light around the block. Pattie relished the possibility of being stopped by a red traffic light where she usually enticed bemused motorists into a drag race in her formidable, little car.

She called it the *Bean Pod* because it was green and carried Beans inside and had one of her design artists paint the name onto its round rear end for motorists to view when she left them in the dust. Drivers often started up conversations at the next set of traffic lights to find out what on earth lay beneath its bonnet!

With such a powerful engine, the interior of the car was always hot. Its saving grace was a small stand-up fan, fixed dubiously to the dashboard. The fan's revolutions and whine kept pace with the engine revs, and I often pleaded with Pattie to take her foot off the accelerator in case the entire apparatus whirled through the windscreen!

A treble blast of the *Bean Pod's* foghorn hooter confirmed her arrival at the school gate and once the dust settled, she emerged wearing something fabulous like a leopard print skirt with a black sweater, red scarf and knee-high boots. Her wild auburn hair was usually squeezed into a slightly askew black Donovan cap and Ringo Star strutted below her on a lead, his pink ears blown back by the dashboard fan. Our friends Annie and Laura thought the excitement of it all was fabulous, but Christianne and I often snuck out from behind the school walls with our pudding bowl hats pulled down over our brows.

Twice a week, after sports activities I walked down to my grandmother's flat in Selous Avenue, from where Pattie would collect me after work. Christianne didn't play any sport because of her bad ears and usually caught the bus home or spent the afternoon with Annie or Laurie on those days.

My Gran, Veronica, was in her late eighties with hardly any grey hair on her head. She was such a devout Catholic that she could say the priest's words at Mass, as well as the responses – in Latin! With the sound of the Convent's lunchtime bell she scurried downstairs every day of the week to capture the flow of schoolgirls trudging past her flat to the bus stops.

"Have you told your mother you love her today?" She asked whoever she managed to nab.

It was a lovely reminder to those who had, but an awkward moment for those who hadn't. Most of them knew her by name and received a proud smile and a pat on the shoulder for the correct answer. A double tap for the wrong answer was a gentle reminder for you to tell your mother when you got home from school. If you escaped Gran at the one o' clock bell you could be captured at five o'clock, when she walked past the school gate to attend evening Mass at the Salisbury Cathedral. Schoolgirls used to come up to me at breaktime to report that they'd bumped into "your grandmother" again.

My studious Aunt Maureen lived with Gran and the weekly bombardment of their combined pearls of wisdom was always interesting. Gran's favourite 'pearl' was the importance in life of the "three R's: reading, writing and arithmetic," but she usually digressed from the subjects with stories about her own life which she felt were just as educational.

"I survived both World Wars in Britain, you know, and we were only allowed one egg a week!" she recalled, waving a Second World War food rationing book in the air.

"Yes, Gran, you told me last week."

Her St John's Ambulance field kit was one of her favourite items to discuss. The black metal box was opened every visit, and each piece of rusty medical equipment inside was explained in detail. Stories about her evacuation to Wales and nights spent in bomb shelters during the Blitz, usually followed.

When story time was over, Gran returned to her rocking chair where she fervently knitted blankets for the poor and Aunt Maureen happily took over with her own favourite subjects. If there was an up-and-coming agricultural show, she usually placed a large piece of paper on the dining room table next to a fruit bowl or vase of flowers and would ask me to draw it. She enjoyed submitting artwork to home industry competitions on behalf of all her nieces and nephews. If there weren't any competitions on the go dusty grammar books surfaced and she would test me on French verbs which was always a tricky time. Having spent her early childhood in France, she loved the language and had hopes of producing her own French dictionary. I found Gran's lessons more captivating, but Maureen's gentle manner got me to do more than just World War II history.

Every year without fail, Veronica knitted Pope John Paul II a balaclava, mittens and a scarf in the papal colours. They were finished to the highest standard, wrapped in brown paper and parcel-posted to the Vatican in time for Easter Sunday celebrations. We were always surprised when the parcel reached its destination and often wondered if the Pope found her gifts useful or just a peculiar annual bundle from an odd woman in Africa. Either way, he replied to her with a papal blessing or a thank you card, which instantly became the talk of Salisbury's Catholic Society. The congregation gathered around Veronica after Mass each time a new card arrived, in the hope of touching something His Holiness might have handled. Although Gran followed his movements closely on television, she never spotted him wearing any of her lovingly made gifts, but that didn't deter her from knitting up a storm yet again the following year.

During this time, Macy's Department Store launched a loyalty campaign that issued green stamps as rewards for buying from them. The stamps were stuck into a coupon book which, when full, could be redeemed for discounts on new purchases. We called Veronica's collection of papal blessings and thank you cards her *green stamps for heaven*, which she could redeem at the Pearly Gates for discounted access if required. *Green stamps* became a family catchphrase for good deeds and the more stamps earned through life, the greater your chances of making it to heaven.

On Fridays, we didn't go to Gran's flat, nor did Pattie pick us up in the *Bean Pod* from school. The driver of the one o' clock ZUPCO bus home to Borrowdale was a fastidious timekeeper and Christianne and I had to sprint to catch it in time. Gran still managed to capture us on the pavement outside her flat with her usual question.

"It's us, Gran!"

"Yes dears, even more reason to ask if you have told your mother that you love her today," she replied, giving us a peck on the cheek.

****

11

At first light, Mistake walked us to Debbie and Hans' cottage. They were delighted with our new plans and after confirming that our lodge was free for a few more days, Debbie cancelled our seats on the boat transfer. If we couldn't get Jules' medicine to the Ume in time, Hans would take us across the Lake in his boat, but Debbie felt confident that we would be able to sort it out.

Wonder then took us to the anthill to phone our pharmacy in Harare. They were happy to help but would only fax the repeat prescription because an email was open to fraud. After studying the national register, they couldn't identify any pharmacies that made use of a fax machine in our vicinity. We would have to phone them back after some investigations and Wonder took us back to Debbie and Hans to explain our predicament. Debbie immediately sent Mistake on a mission to the employees' compound, hoping that one of the 1000 residents had the information that we needed. We chewed nails for an hour, before he came running up the path towards us waving a piece of paper in the air.

"Mrs Makumbe had malaria, the chemist she used has a fax!" He beamed.

We danced around the piece of paper whistling and ululating like we had just won the lottery.

"You're welcome," he shouted, running down the path back to our lodge.

Unfortunately, when the euphoria died down, his piece of paper revealed that Mrs Makumbe's chemist was at Kariba

Heights, 57 kilometres back across the lake but all was not lost if we could find a way of getting the medicine delivered to the Ume River.

The boat transfer was only due back in a week, which would be too late. Wonder suggested we use his cousin's taxi service in the Binga communal area, a hundred kilometres away on the treacherous Siyakobvu dirt road, but that would cost too much. Hans radioed the Lake Captain to check if any tourist houseboats were heading in our direction, but none were coming up this far.

"What about the Transporter?" asked Debbie.

With Bushy on our heels, Hans walked us around to the deeper side of the harbour where a rusty 40-tonne vessel with two 210 horsepower Cummins diesel engines was moored. The Transporter crossed the lake from Kariba and carried a lifeline of fresh food and commodities for the people living in the Ume area. A tiny brown packet of medicine could easily be lost within its bowels, but it was worth a try. Crucially, it was about to leave for Kariba and would be back in the Ume tomorrow morning. We left the Transporter for the anthill, and I gave the pharmacy the fax number that they required. Hans radioed a work colleague in Kariba who agreed to collect the pills from the pharmacy in the Heights and deliver them to the Transporter when it arrived in the harbour later that afternoon.

Jules poured celebratory drinks while Hans tossed pork sausages on the braai, gloating at the success of our bush network.

"Ume (A) is playing an important football match on Saturday, you'll now be able to watch it," Hans said.

"You'll have time to visit the junior school as well," added Debbie.

Wonder walked us back to the lodge after lunch and while Jules got stuck into a Mega crossword puzzle, I returned to my laptop, smiling at the thought of having more time in the Ume to continue with Pattie's story.

****

By October 1977, the guerrilla war tactics of hit-and-run attacks on Rhodesian farms had escalated. Civilians of every race were targeted, women and children included. The country was stunned by the murder of Natasha Glenny, a six-month-old baby ripped from her childminder's back and bayoneted to death at the Highlands Wattle Estate in Chipinga.

Pieter and Bin sold their farm in Marandellas and moved further away from the hot spot of the Mozambique border in the northeast and bought a farm in the south of the country, closer to the friendlier South African border. Bin's sister Angela came to visit shortly after they had moved in but flew into Harare first to see Veronica and Maureen. Pieter was away on a six-week army call up, so it was the perfect opportunity for all the sisters to get together and visit Bin on the farm. Margaret drove us all down there with her children Elizabeth and James.

The farmstead was attacked on the first night. Bullets riddled the walls and by some miracle, one RPG rocket flew over the house and the second one was a dud which got tangled in the perimeter security fence and didn't explode. For our own protection, Christianne and I were shoved into a windowless pantry with our cousins while Margaret, Pattie and Angela armed the doors after a quick lesson on how to use a gun. Bin radioed Agric-Alert to raise the alarm with neighbouring farms and our attackers were chased off by a squadron of Rhodesian troops who were on reconnaissance nearby. The farmstead was battered but no one was hurt. When Pieter returned from call-up, he stomped around the house, slamming doors, furious that anyone had dared to threaten his family and was grateful that his sisters-in-law had been at Bin's side that night. It was the closest we'd got to the war so far and life bumbled on.

In 1978, the massacre of nine missionaries and their four young children in Vumba deeply affected Pattie. She joined several professional organisations and hoped that the power of public relations and publicity could make a peaceful difference to the war. 2700 civilians had been murdered and villagers in rural areas bore the brunt. Cattle were slaughtered or hamstrung, homes and grain stores burnt to the ground. She became Chairlady of Women for Rhodesia, an apolitical organisation dedicated to the spread of accurate information on the war. Her hard-hitting articles appeared in newspapers and magazines exposing the murder of innocent civilians on both sides of the conflict. She sent a five-page telegram to the governments of Britain, Canada, and Australia. In one of the paragraphs, she wrote:

"We feel the atrocities being committed have gone far enough and we should get people in other countries to relate to the pain, anguish and sorrow of the people here."

Her telegrams went unanswered. Government ministries weren't willing to offer support in any form to an unrecognised government, but she had to do something no matter how small. She published hundreds of Christmas cards with a picture of four young children of different races on the front and hoped it would be posted worldwide to increase awareness of the atrocities. The inscription inside read:

"While the world hurls abuse, while politicians foil with words, we the ordinary people of Rhodesia, are caught in the crossfire of real bullets."

As Chairlady of Women for Peace and the Catholic Women's League she gathered powerful women of all races and creeds around her dining-room table to discuss peaceful ways of ending the war.

At a lunch of 100 members of the Business and Professional Women's Club for its International Week, Pattie spoke of:

"...the tremendous work done in the development of laws and regulations relating to the place of women in society. We have no need for a militant approach to change. No riots, no bra-burning, just research, reports, discussions, and quiet victories without fanfares of triumph. Women are drawn together in a common desire to protect their families. Because our common bonds outweigh our common differences, we cut across barriers and accept the similarities in our hopes, joys and fears within the colourful variations of cultural groups."

Mathewman, Banks, and Tholet promoted her to Advertising Executive; high-profile clients like Air Rhodesia, Beverley Building Society, South African Airways and *Illustrated Life of Rhodesia* were added to her portfolio. The Prime Minister's son-in-law, Clem Tholet, was her fiery Artistic Director, who produced catchy advertising jingles and patriotic folk songs. His most famous song, *Rhodesians Never Die*, epitomised the defiance of UDI and got the blood running of every 18-year-old in army uniform.

Pattie and Clem worked well together, but tensions rose around deadlines when she felt it necessary to plaster his desk with post-It type reminders of the cut-off dates. It was a constant source of irritation to Clem, and I was in her office one day after school when he stormed in after a boozy client lunch and shoved as many of her notes as possible into his mouth, chewing furiously before swallowing the lot. From then on, Pattie wrote all her reminders on rice paper; "more palatable," she told him.

On a salary of $750 per month life gradually got easier for our family and Pattie booked a holiday for us at a self-catering cottage in Kariba Heights. During the war, all road travel outside the city centres was done with a military convoy but that didn't deter her.

The *Bean Pod* was loaded with flasks of tea and treats of ginger biscuits and Willard's salt and vinegar crisps. Several packets of Jelly Baby sweets were stuffed into the glove compartment and Ringo Star barked each time Pattie became animated and ripped off one of their heads. She felt they were the best remedy for moments of stress and our pantry was fully stocked with them since her divorce. The small wooden shelf in the boot of the Morris was filled to bursting with a shared suitcase of clothes, a spare wheel, groceries, and a dog basket.

The convoy left at 6am and the army officer registering travellers winced at the sight of a woman and two young girls in a noisy old car, with an equally loud pink dog! He felt none of these factors fulfilled the need for stealth and speed on his convoy, but Pattie's enthusiastic description of the inner workings of the *Bean Pod*, and our excitement, soon won him over. After registering our names, he directed us to the safest spot in the middle of the convoy but didn't hide his irritation when Pattie asked for Ringo Star to be registered as well.

"He's a family treasure, Officer!"

"Have you got a weapon?" he grunted.

"Sir, Ringo Star is our weapon," she replied.

She had already noticed that our car was the only one without a gun of some sort sticking out the side window but didn't make a thing of it. When the officer left to sign in another vehicle, grumbling "make sure you keep up", Ringo Star saw him off with a bark and Pattie revved the engine, sending the stand-up fan into a cheeky whirl.

Two hours later, as the sun rose over the Ayrshire Hills, the convoy made a pit stop in the farming town of Banket. The army was on high alert because Robert Mugabe was born in the district and the area was a hot spot for his loyal freedom fighters.

"Let's have a large cup of tea, it fixes everything, you know!" Pattie suggested.

The *Bean Pod* had impressed the army officer, particularly going up the steep hills of the Great Dyke Mountain Pass, but the strain on the engine made the heat inside unbearable. The break at the Banket Hotel would give us the chance to cool down and escape Edith Piaf, whose songs had been belting out from a cassette player, competing ferociously with the whine of the stand-up fan. Known as the *Little Sparrow*, Edith had remained one of Pattie's favourite singers over the years. The complexities and contradictions of her hit song *Non je ne regrette rien*, epitomising my mother's emotions at the time. Every syllable was heard to the last: over, and over, and over again!

We left Banket with a broomstick protruding from the passenger window, Pattie having convinced the hotel manager to part with it. Ringo Star barked at the intrusion, and we giggled at the absurdity, making occasional mock machine gun sounds out of the window on open stretches of road.

When we arrived at the holiday cottage four hours later Pattie limped to the front door. The double clutch and sprung seats of the *Bean Pod* had taken its toll on her hip replacement. She made light of it by using the "lovely" broom handle as a walking stick.

The Rhodesian army vigorously patrolled Kariba Heights and the dam wall to keep its hydroelectric power station secure from attack. It was comforting to see them on every corner and, together with the broom handle and Ringo Star, we felt perfectly safe.

Each morning, Pattie plotted short adventure walks and made simple things exciting. Searching for unusual insects in a pile of elephant dung with a stick became a treasure hunt and we shrieked with laughter when a chameleon wobbled on the side of the road and turned pink when Ringo gave it a good sniff.

We played protracted games of Monopoly, Cluedo, and Vingt-et-un, which Pattie manipulated to give Christianne and me a turn to win to keep the peace. Our favourite outing was a picnic and evening movie at the open-air cinema where Pattie balanced precariously on an overstuffed cushion to relieve her hip from the discomfort of the stone amphitheatre seats.

"Isn't this just lovely girls? Look, not a cloud in sight," she commented.

After the movie, we walked home in the dark with the rest of the audience scattering in every direction. A short way from our cottage Ringo Star stopped dead in his tracks, growling into a dark area of bush near the roadside. The broom handle once again metamorphosed into a rifle and rose to Pattie's shoulder. Ringo Star almost lost his voice and had to be pulled away from his stand so we could quick-march home. We learnt from the village chatter the following morning that a leopard had been on the prowl and Ringo Star had probably saved us from being an early dinner!

On September 8th, 1978, Air Rhodesia Viscount flight 825 Hunyani was shot down by nationalist fighters. It fell from the sky shortly after take-off from Kariba, on route to Salisbury. It was carrying 56 civilians. 18 survived the crash but 10 were shot on the ground. Pattie lost friends and work colleagues and organised press releases and condolence messages on behalf of her client. The build-up to the memorial service was intense and the Very Reverend JR da Costa's "Silence is deafening" speech rang through the Anglican Cathedral of Saint Mary and All Saints. Five months later, Air Rhodesia flight 827 Umniati was also shot down, another 59 civilians were killed.

When Woolworths Department store was bombed in August 1977 the bush war had reached the capital city. In

December 1978, the Shell BP fuel depot in Salisbury was bombed and 11 storage tanks burst spectacularly into flames. Black smoke blew 180 metres into the air, blanketing the city and the Dominican Convent School where I was hiding under my desk with Laura.

As the school alarm rang out, children emerged from their classrooms in orderly lines following their teachers into the school quadrangle. Using a PA system, our Headmistress, Sister Mary Pancratius, gave the command for the entire Middle and Senior School to follow behind her and evacuate the grounds. She glided towards Fourth Street, genuflecting at the Grotto of Mother Mary before inserting an enormous key into the main school gate.

Hundreds of school children covered in soot, lined the kerb waiting to be collected. Horns honked and parents shouted out for their children as every fire engine in the city sped past towards the blaze with sirens blaring. Above it all, my sister and I heard the discernible rumble of the *Bean Pod* which came screeching to a stop at boiling point outside the school gate. Ringo Star's head was out of the passenger window looking more comical than usual with only two pink rings around his eyes having escaped the soot. His voice was hoarse from barking, but he seemed pleased that he'd helped clear the way for Pattie to jump every traffic light to get to us.

On the way home we stopped in on Gran and Maureen, who refused to leave their flat. They felt perfectly safe covering their windows and doors with blankets and towels "we did the same in 1940, during the Blitz of London," Gran said. The *Bean Pod's* furious race away from smoke over-torqued the twin carburettor engine which sadly never started up again once we got home.

School was shut for a week and when it reopened, a dull Ford Anglia delivered us quietly to the school gate. An emergency law was introduced making it compulsory for pupils to print their names on both sides of their school suitcases to eliminate them as a bomb threat. I never understood the reasoning behind it, but the bomb squad would be called if a name wasn't visible.

In early puberty everything embarrassed me, including my delightfully long name, which now appeared in bold white capital letters on both sides of my suitcase for all to see. Laura thought it was hysterical, especially when we caught the bus home, and I made her walk right next to me to hide one side of my suitcase. A strategically placed sports bag usually hid the other side. With teenage belligerence, I considered breaking the rules by painting over the 37 letters. Losing all my homework to a small explosion by the bomb squad also had great appeal.

The fuel depot fire raged for five days, and smoke could be seen from 50 kilometres away. It was a tactical hit that left Rhodesia without fuel to fight a war and was a financial blow to Ian Smith's isolated government. A ceasefire was called, and with pre-independence negotiations on the table, an interim government was formed. Just as Bishop Abel Muzorewa became the first black Prime Minister of the newly named Zimbabwe-Rhodesia, Pattie became the first woman to be granted full membership of the Institute of Marketing Management. Marketing was the new buzzword and was not previously considered an intellectual profession. She thought it a powerful, exciting, and progressive tool. In her acceptance speech she said:

"I think it will be quite some time before women obtain equality of job and salary in this country, but they have had the ideal platform for growth over the last few years and I think it is a great pity that more have not seized the opportunity. Emancipation is not demanding rights – it is development of what you have to offer society to the point that the rights are inevitable."

In June 1979 names were mercifully removed from our

school suitcases, and by December, the Lancaster House Agreement was signed. In April 1980, white rule ended, and the Republic of Zimbabwe was born. The moderate Methodist minister, Canaan Banana, became its first President, more as a transitional figurehead than anything else. A new law was pushed through making it illegal to mock his name. Robert Mugabe became the Prime Minister and set about joining all political parties together into a single party state, whether they wanted to or not. Banana split after ruling for seven years and Mugabe became President.

The name of our capital city, Salisbury changed to Harare; spellings of towns and cities were altered to reflect local pronunciation. Buildings and streets that had been named after Rhodesian pioneers and colonial icons were replaced with the names of pertinent contributors to the Liberation Struggle.

These weren't the only names to change in our lives.

****

It was well past midnight when I turned off my laptop and the sticky moths left in search of another light source followed by the nightjars and bats. I fell asleep listening to crickets, owls and frogs which sounded just as content as I was to be in the wilds of the Ume River.

12

The morning air was fresh, and a cool breeze drifted over the balcony. Through the binoculars, I could see the Transporter chomping through the water towards the harbour. It's billowing exhaust smoke heralded the arrival of Jules' medicine and, by the look of it, an awful lot else. Being a Friday, the vessel was carrying commuters returning from Kariba for the weekend as well as vital commodities for the community. Football supporters attending tomorrow's important league fixture, added to the weekly load.

Excited crowds gathered on the shoreline to help offload drums of fuel, paraffin, maize meal and huge mounds of vegetables that couldn't be grown in the Ume heat. A decrepit Peugeot station wagon with enormous sacks of maputi[10] strapped to the roof rack, disembarked first. The driver had his head out of the window, watching the wheels closely as he steered the vehicle across two warped wooden planks to shore. Commuters carrying their weekly wages were greeted by family members, some with babies strapped to their backs. Drunken football supporters rolled off last and opposition fans jeered.

By the time Jules and I came downstairs for breakfast, a tiny brown packet was sitting on the dining room table, glorified by a few stems of freshly cut pampas grass. Both Wonder and Mistake pointed out the medicine with pride.

"Are you coming to my football match tomorrow?"

---

10. Traditional sun-dried maize kernel that is roasted and salted.

Mistake asked.

"Wouldn't miss it for the world!" I replied.

Wonder directed us to the sideboard where leftover bread rolls had replaced the rusks in the wicker basket. A sprig of red bougainvillea was draped over the apricot jam to make it look more interesting. A pot of maize meal porridge steamed in the hostess trolley, enough to feed an army. Wonder was disappointed by the rudimentary cooking skills on display, but it was a fine breakfast none-the-less.

"Are you playing in the football match?" I asked.

"I am going to church," he replied, with a discerning look.

The entire crocodile farm was buzzing with excitement about the game, but my promise to watch Mistake play football instead of perhaps going to church didn't seem to hold much water with Wonder. It was, however, a critical game and Ume (A) needed to beat fierce rival and current league leader Chilala (A) Football Club to go on top. Mistake was strutting around the garden doing his chores with his chest puffed out ready to put on show of his skills tomorrow. With our stay in the Ume extended, Jules and I were in no rush to do much for the rest of the day. I didn't even turn on my laptop, which made a pleasant change.

Hans came to collect us early the next morning and walked us through the Jesse bush to the Ume airstrip where part of the runway apron had been transformed into a football field. The moveable goals and simple ground markings suggested that league fixtures were slotted around flight timetables to avoid an incoming Cessna or two forcing a time-out!

It was a breezy day and clouds of dust from the airstrip followed packs of supporters arriving from every direction. Cyclists, riding double, raced towards the field. Families from the employee's compound arrived early to get the best seats at the edge of the field. Mothers laid out cotton wraps on the floor, reserving play spaces for their babies. Several ashen looking fans piled out of battered VW Kombis having survived the treacherous Siyakobvu dirt road from Binga. Some supporters scrambled out of dodgy looking dugout canoes that had made it across the Ume River and tied up in the harbour.

Vendors carrying cardboard trays of cold drinks, sweets, maputi and hard-boiled eggs whizzed through the crowds haggling for an early sale. Sadza[11] and relish bubbled in cauldrons behind each set of goals and the delicious smell wafted through the air, enticing spectators to eat.

A shiny wooden bench from the Ume Junior School was wedged into the middle of the Ume (A) supporters' area for us to sit on. Employees strutted around Hans and Debbie shaking hands and turning their backs to reveal their football jersey numbers, each promising to score the winning goal. A group of well-rounded cheerleaders with babies strapped to their backs danced and shook maracas in a line in front of us. Their enthusiasm doubled when Jules and I joined them for a couple of dances which led to bursts of ululation, vigorous hand slapping and hip bumps so exuberant that they almost knocked us to the ground!

The game started with a deafening roar and a huge cloud of dust. Each time Mistake touched the ball he checked to see that we were watching which we acknowledged with two-fingered whistles, especially when he was fouled. Through all the dust I caught a glimpse of him passing the ball to a striker, who scored. Both players ran into the supporters' area with shirts over their heads, imitating premier league heroes. We leapt on top of the bench for height advantage and ululated as Mistake pranced by.

Across the airstrip, a baboon made off with a booty of

---

11. A staple food of boiled maize meal

stolen tomatoes and was chased up a tree by a stick-wielding vendor. In the shade below, a group of white-gowned apostolic worshippers sang their hearts out to compete with the noise from the football field. I tried to pick out Wonder, but the sea of white cloth made it difficult, and my attention was diverted by the shrill sound of the referee's whistle calling for a time-out after two players collided. When the dust settled, a man lay on the ground, surrounded by players. For a terrible moment I thought it was Mistake, but I spotted him by the goals, glugging down some water from a tin cup.

A hushed crowd watched a beefy nurse from the Ume clinic take to the field in her whites. The injured player was from the opposition team and his ankle had been badly sprained in the clash. It was a relief that nothing was broken, emergency care was limited this far across the Lake. The nurse applied a thick bandage, dosed him up with a couple of large white pills and he winced in pain as two teammates shouldered him off the pitch. The Transporter was only leaving in the morning, so he would have to suffer the night before a more thorough examination could be done at Kariba District Hospital. In the meantime, more large white pills and several scuds[12] of local beer would suffice for pain control.

During the lull in crowd noise, songs of praise from Wonder's congregation drifted across the airstrip pinching the consciences of a few football-watching heathens until a pleased looking substitute took to the field and cheers erupted again. The game was a tightly fought, physical encounter. I was surprised more players weren't carried off the field. Chilala (A) equalized from a brilliant corner kick and the game ended in a draw. Disappointed crowds, covered in fine

---

12. 1 litre of beer made from maize grits and sorghum fermented with yeast, sold in brown plastic bottle

dust, dispersed in every direction, dissecting the result as they went. Vendors packed up their wares and our wooden bench was carried off on the head of one of the cheerleaders. The goalposts were removed, and the field lines were brushed away in time for the next flight. Only the worshippers remained behind, harmonizing songs of praise under the shade of a mopane tree.

Mistake gleamed with pride on the walk back to the lodge. We all had a lot to say about his various moves and plays during the game and stopped for a moment to examine the photographs I'd taken. He identified teammates and star players and promised to give Chilala (A) a good thrashing when they met again. We were so involved in conversation that we passed the buffalo and hippo danger zones without a second glance.

After a quick dip in the pool to rinse off the dust, I returned to my laptop and just as I sat down a fish eagle swooped into the fig tree. Silhouetted against the afternoon sun, it threw back its head and called out the end of another glorious day on the river. I felt like doing the same.

****

13

The 1980s brought with it the hopes and fears of new governance in Zimbabwe. Bin and Pieter emigrated to Warmbaths in South Africa, but as one of Pattie's sisters left another returned when Angela moved back to Harare. I was inconsolable when Laura and her family left the country as well: we had been joined at the hip for 11 years.

In 1981, Pattie went to Richard Taunton's cabaret show birthday party at his farm in Norton. During one of the skits, a 61-year-old man appeared on stage as a singing waitress and Pattie was instantly intrigued. Their relationship blossomed secretly and rapidly, and it came as a complete surprise when Christianne and I were dragged off to dinner for an official introduction to Mr Norman Pink - a mechanical engineer from England who'd worked his passage to Africa on a converted mine sweeper in the late 1940s. He had a posh accent and wore a smart suit with a handkerchief pressed into the top pocket next to a perfectly hung necktie. Shiny cufflinks twinkled from the end of his arms and his silver head of heavily brylcreemed hair was perfectly parted to one side and glistened in the low lights of his orderly home.

A strange device called a lazy Susan was centred on the dining room table and carried mature jars of mustard, Rosella jelly and other condiments which he considered vital to a meal. Pattie gave me several lady-like kicks under the table when I questioned why they couldn't simply be passed around by hand like normal.

It had been several years since a man had been in our

lives, other than Ringo Star, and our mother was behaving peculiarly. They already had terms of endearment for each other. Norman was called "Mister" and she was his "Lovebug" and both blushed when the names slipped into the conversation by mistake.

To make friends, Norman asked simple questions.

"What are your favourite sports, girls?"

Christianne replied that she didn't play any because of her bad ears! After a pause and another gulp of red wine for courage, he began a lengthy monologue about the "splendid" game of cricket, marvelling about the upset victory when Zimbabwe beat the West Indies and Australia in the ICC World Cup qualifiers. We had no idea what he was talking about, particularly his detailed account of the bowling statistics of a cricket great called John Traicos, who had a right arm off spin just like the lazy Susan, it seemed.

"Gosh Mister, how lovely!" Lovebug commented.

She hadn't watched a cricket game in her life, but it spurred Norman on. He asked about favourite school subjects and was pleased to hear that art was one of them; his daughter, Mandy, had studied Art and Design. He was perturbed that neither of us mentioned maths, it was a subject in which he revelled, while we collectively avoided it. His son, Clive, had graduated with honours in pure maths at university. When I could get a word in, I described how my maths teacher pinned me on the back of the head with the blackboard duster when I went wrong with an equation on the board. Norman immediately enquired what the equation was, eager to solve it for me. He wasn't the least bit interested in my Shona language classes which had been rapidly introduced to our post-independence school curriculum.

"French is a more useful language, Liza," he said, abbreviating my name.

I continued with a description of our Shona teacher, Mr

Patsanza, and how he got us to animate vocabulary as a way of imprinting new words on our minds.

"Famba!" I shouted, actioning the verb - *to walk* with a strut around the table.

Mr Patsanza's methods were great fun, and I progressed far quicker with his teaching methods than with the flying blackboard dusters of Pythagoras enthusiasts. Norman thought my animations were hilarious and in stark contrast to the strict teaching of Dulwich College where he went to school.

"My name is Lissie, by the way," I explained with teenage belligerence, "spelt with an 's' not a 'z'."

Lovebug whispered to him that it sounded softer.

His protracted dissection of the magnificent mechanical engineering beneath the bonnet of his automatic BMW was both incomprehensible and exhausting, but he found Pattie's description of the *Bean Pod's* twin carburettors interesting, which pleased her no end. He refrained from commenting on the Ford Anglia by diverting the conversation to the colossal pumpkins that he grew for competitions. Growing a small one was a miracle to us!

After another glass of wine, Norman broke into song, which was startling. Pattie joined in when she knew the words, but his Latin school song flummoxed us all and was sung with such fervour that we were left spellbound.

Our mother had fallen in love and Christianne and I would have to share her going forward. Opposites had certainly attracted, and they laughed at each other's differences all the time. A neat, methodical English gentleman with a flamboyant, adventurous advertising executive changed our teenage years for the good. Driving home from dinner that night, Pattie gingerly asked what we thought of him.

"He's different, but ok, Mum. You had better learn the words to that Latin song though!" Her relief was obvious.

The following week, Norman came to Chancing Lane for the first home visit and an introduction to Ringo Star which went much better than expected. Instead of going on the attack, Ringo curled up on Norman's lap, relieved to have another man in the house to assist with guard duties.

Pattie and Norman married in 1983 on the front lawn of our new family home which sat on top of a seven-acre hill, overlooking Borrowdale Brook. Many of Harare's personalities attended the wedding, Richard and Dawn Taunton, Godfrey Majonga, Wynne Wilson, Wynne Hooper, Tilly Jackson, Jane Chavanduka, and Kiki Divaris, were among them. Our guests sat out in the open on ribboned plastic chairs that had been wedged into the grassy hilltop to prevent a tumble during the ceremony.

The tables were simply decorated with honeysuckle and jasmine plucked from the garden hedges, and a scattering of pink jellybeans symbolized the union. Hymns roared out over the valley, led from the front by Norman in his Dulwich school choir baritone while Pattie competed in descant. They looked "splendid", but I had been forced into a bridesmaid dress and felt uncomfortable. Christianne and our cousin, Elizabeth, looked radiant, far more at ease with all the puffy lacy stuff. We spent the entire service muting giggles as the ancient priest forgot most of the words and had to be prompted by Pattie. He had been dragged out of the church woodworks to perform the un-Catholic second marriage ceremony. In the eyes of her church, Pattie had broken a holy sacrament by divorcing my father and could no longer receive Holy Communion, the core of her religion. I found this a bitter pill to swallow on her behalf; Ken had left us not the other way around. I questioned Catholicism from that moment on.

Pattie on the other hand, remained devout and went to Mass every Sunday without fail. She became actively involved in charity projects at St Gerard's Church down the road and attended every one of its social events. Her new name, Pattie Pink, appeared on church notices appealing for donations and volunteers for a variety of causes. The notices were read out after Mass which made the service longer than necessary but afterwards it became a family tradition to drive to Pomona Bakery and buy a freshly baked French loaf. When we got home, the corners were cut off and given to Ringo Star as his part of the treat and the remainder was cut into equal fours. Each piece was filled with a fried egg, crispy bacon and topped with a blob of HP Sauce, found in a bottle swirling around the lazy Susan that had followed Norman from his bachelor pad. It's a taste from my childhood I will never forget.

Christianne and I were given the option to change our surname.

"From Bean to Pink? No thanks, Mum!" I answered quickly.

Esher Close was Pattie's dream home, with a spectacular view overlooking a brook with fields of wheat and cabbages and the Murewa hills beyond. Norman gave in easily to her choice of home when he saw how much she loved it, but structurally it was long, badly built, perched on top of a granite hill with crooked doors, leaking pipes and windows that didn't close easily. It would be a mammoth task to bring it up to his high engineering standards. Lovebug thought it had character and the best view in the country.

Before starting on the house repairs, Norman planted the pumpkin seeds for the Harare Men's Club annual competition. As the veg mutated, Pattie worried that it might break loose from its vine, roll down her hill and kill someone; she imagined the headlines *'Locals threatened by deadly pumpkin!'* which would probably be a first, but Norman built a retaining wall to allay her fears and to keep his precious veg and the neighbourhood safe.

Next on his agenda was a mechanic's pit to service our vehicle, whose engine he felt had been severely mistreated. He couldn't dig down into the granite hillside easily so came up with a plan to use the gradient and build two walls jutting out from it at right angles. They were the exact width of a vehicle apart and the correct height for him to toil underneath without straining his back. Detailed progress reports were explained at dinner every night.

"Good Heavens, Mister, you are clever," Lovebug commented.

She immediately planted a row of bougainvillea and honeysuckle to conceal its structure from her beautiful hillside.

When he summoned the Ford Anglia for a service, nerves of steel were required to reverse it over the pit with what felt like a canyon below. Pattie usually abandoned the car at the start of the ramp, yanking the hand brake up to its maximum and placing a small stone behind the back wheel for good measure. He would smile at her girlish fears and reverse over the pit at speed, stopping a few inches from the edge.

He kept meticulous notes on each vehicle in the glove box detailing fuel usage, tyre pressure and oil changes. A good dosing of wax polish on Saturdays ensured that we arrived at Sunday Mass gleaming.

With a home, and a husband in support, Pattie left Mathewman, Banks and Tholet and joined Jill Baker and Associates before opening her own company called PIC Films. She was finally in control of the script writing, editing, and producing of her own creative ideas for television and radio. It may have taken her over 30 years, but her dream had come true. Staff from the Zimbabwe Broadcasting Company found the adjustment from Mrs Bean to Mrs Pink difficult, so they called her Sweet Pea. She signed her Christmas newsletter that year from the *Pink Beans* and thought it had a lovely marketing ring to it.

Ringo Star lived to the mature age of fifteen. The older and blinder he got, the more defensive he became. He spent his last days barking at the Wellington boots left outside the back door by the gardener. When he retired from his guard duties, he fell asleep in his basket, satisfied that his family had been left in good hands. Pattie prayed to St Francis to keep her family treasure in his arms and buried him under the hibiscus bush outside her bedroom, so he could keep an eye on her.

****

14

The Transporter left the Ume for Kariba at first light. The winds were up again and watching its bow rise into a bright blue sky and crash down onto white horses, I thought of the injured footballer and all the hungover supporters who would be on board. They would all need a good dose of large white pills to cope with the rough journey ahead of them. Mistake had given the injured player a piggy-back across the two wobbly planks onto the boat and said the man was in good spirits, which was not surprising considering the number of beers he had managed to guzzle.

The gentle sounds of Africa returned once the Transporter was out of hearing distance until the sheep arrived for their morning drink. Twin lambs Shawn and Stewart beelined for the budding strelitzia again, scraping their feet at a makeshift fence that Mistake had erected for its protection. Edith stomped over to my desk and growled for her usual treats, but I could only scavenge a crust from the bread bin to share out.

Wonder's voice was hoarse from singing and he looked downcast with the breakfast display. He had spread out the last of the condiments and draped them with yesterday's sprig of red bougainvillea to fill the table. The hostess trolley held the final batch of maize meal porridge, so we would not starve, but would need to go fishing later.

After breakfast, we asked him to walk us across to Debbie and Hans to see if we could borrow a few toiletries that we were running short of. To our surprise, he suggested we visit the small shop in the employees' compound instead. We were unaware of its existence and Wonder agreed to take us there immediately.

The tin shack shimmered beneath the African sun along a bustling dirt path in the centre of the compound. Puffs of dust followed children who were kicking a small football made from compressed plastic bags. Their mothers stood in circles gossiping in the Ume heat, vendors shouted out prices, dogs barked, and baboons leapt from the ground to the trees, armed with spoils from an overflowing rubbish pit.

Jules named the shop, "The Boulevard" which was a fine name for a tin shack that offered a variety of brightly coloured household vitals like toothpaste, soap, long-life milk and mobile phone data. It also sold packets of maputi, scuds of the local beer and mounds of sundried fish, bugs and insects, which looked tricky to swallow.

Speaking to the shop owner in Tonga, Wonder gave him our order and the first item to appear over the counter was an enormous five-hundred-gram chunk of bright pink soap. It took two hands to receive and reeked of cinnamon, probably to disguise its carbolic composition. The toothpaste tube and milk carton, mercifully, looked to be original in a sealed box, as did the shampoo. Only the half-jack of brandy looked a little dodgy, but the seal was unbroken. I added a packet of maputi to the order at the last minute for Edith's family, they possibly had the teeth for it!

After purchasing the colourful necessities, Wonder agreed to take us back to the lodge via the anthill so I could phone the respite home, but Pattie was in a flower arranging class and couldn't speak to me. The image of her trying to create some sort of posy brought a smile to my face as she was never very good at that but at least she was participating in some of the activities.

Hans was walking up from the boat mooring when we arrived at the lodge. He had been at work since three in the morning which was normal practice as the season edged into September and the rising heat stopped work before lunchtime. The empty fuel tank that he was carrying banged against his knee sending a Goliath heron into flight from the grassy edge.

"Bushy and I aren't coming fishing today; we are watching Tri-Nations' rugby this afternoon instead. I've put fuel in the tank, take the boat out yourselves," he said handing over the keys.

Edith and her family gobbled up the maputi that I scattered at the gate as a diversion and Gertrude snatched a few pieces from my hand before sashaying back down to the shade of the fig tree. Mistake placed a much lighter cooler box in Bushy's spot under the console while I primed the fuel pump, lowered the engine, and started the boat on my first attempt. Mistake could tell that the Ume was growing on us and smiled at my confidence as he pushed us out into the water, shouting "You're welcome and tight lines!"

The water level of the lake had dropped overnight, and the hippos had moved from Bird Island to deeper water, which was a relief. The sluice gates had probably been opened to provide meagre amounts of hydroelectric power to the nation. The constant power outages and water shortages in Harare had been forgotten during our stay in the Ume and the thought of returning to it all was not appealing.

We spent the afternoon following the shade around the island, keeping an eye out for the darter chicks and catching a few fish which would please Wonder no end. I'm not sure whether it was the first tot of suspicious looking Boulevard brandy or the feeling of general apathy about returning to Harare, but we started discussing the possibility of moving to the Ume for the simple life. Jules could teach maths at the school, and I could do bird or photographic safaris. Hildah, Scruffy and Muffin would love the bush, although Muffin would need to be restrained from chasing wildlife. She had once chased a combine harvester so a lion would be a piece of cake. We would also have to watch her with Edith: both were strong women who might clash. By the second tot of Boulevard Brandy, we were looking at dates to move!

Ideas and plans were tossed around all afternoon until our thoughts were diverted by several boats speeding past heading towards the Ume harbour. The bush telegraph had received intelligence about Hans and Bushy's open invitation to watch New Zealand play rugby against South Africa at 3pm, with air conditioning!

The bow of a national park's banana boat rose through the waves, crossing from Balabala camp carrying two German clients and a couple of game guides who waved as they passed by. Two New Zealanders from Tashinga camp sped past in a small boat with a cooler box of beer. Their banter about New Zealand thrashing South Africa in this afternoon's game continued until they beached on the shoreline. Jules and I decided that it would be a great game to watch and followed them in, passing several enormous crocodiles eyeing a waterbuck on land.

The Springbok rugby team had been on a losing streak but playing on home turf at the Nelson Mandela Stadium in Port Elizabeth, made the difference. The hard-fought win of 18-5 over New Zealand resulted in several outburst "Nkosi Sikelel' iAfrica[13]" from us and we had a typical Zimbabwean afternoon with strangers who left as friends.

Wonder collected us after the game and was pleased with our catch. There was no need to cook fish tonight as Debbie had already sent across a small chicken for him to roast for

---

13. First line of the South African National Anthem "Lord Bless Africa."

us. He would make a fish pie tomorrow night and use up the last of the potatoes in the tin trunk. On the walk home, we heard lions roaring in the distance which made us pick up the pace but didn't stop the chatter about moving to the Ume, which pleased Wonder even more.

"You could write children's stories, which I could illustrate," Jules suggested.

I hadn't finished one book yet! It was mind boggling and once we were at the lodge, I retreated to the quiet of a very deep bath where the cinnamon soap took on a life of its own! It was impossible to hold with one hand and brutal when dropped onto a body part. The bath water and flannel turned pink in an instant and the suffocating aroma stuck to the walls. I emerged from the bathroom with a pink hue wafting of cinnamon, but the disinfectant in the soap kept the mosquitoes away during a hot, restless night, our minds buzzing with crazy ideas. Was it the Boulevard brandy or were we going bush mad?

The next morning, I asked Mistake to give the soap a good wallop with his best axe to make it more manageable, but I still had a pink glow when I sat down to write!

****

15

PIC Films received a huge boost when Pattie was appointed public relations consultant for the Conservation Trust of Zimbabwe. Its President, John Pile, had been impressed with her punchy scripts and desire to educate through the medium of film. She also had a keen interest in the preservation of Zimbabwe's natural resources and heritage. John looked preserved himself, with an enormous white handlebar moustache, and was hardly seen out of a safari suit, wielding a hefty walking stick. Zimbabwe was independent and free from the shackles of international isolation that had come with UDI. John and Pattie planned to put the country back on the map by producing promotional and educational films.

Pattie agreed to write the scripts and produce and present the films and she commissioned Willie Memper to be her cameraman and film editor. They made a cracking team and travelled the length and breadth of the country, visiting National Parks, Botanical Gardens and Heritage sites capturing their essence. The programmes featured on prime-time television every Sunday evening, when our home buzzed with excitement to see our mother on national TV. Dinner was simple and fast so we wouldn't miss one bit of her 13-week series called *Around the World Zimbabwe*. Mister always commented how beautiful Lovebug looked when she appeared on the screen with a huge smile, wearing a safari jacket with an animal print skirt and a large hat of some sort. She started with her usual opening spiel.

"Hello viewers, here we are at Chipangali Wildlife

Orphanage in Bulawayo..." or "Hello viewers, here we are at the bushman paintings of Domboshawa Hills."

She became a television personality and worked her way into the hearts of Zimbabweans with her sincere, natural presentations. She wrote in her Christmas newsletter that year that *"she was grateful for her life. It was full of adventure."*

The only thing holding her back was the size of her Ford Anglia which was too small to carry all the camera equipment and prone to overheating. She started to use Norman's immaculate BMW more and more and he hid his resignation within the excitement, each time a new film series was approved. Of course, he wanted Lovebug kept safe on her travels, but most of the rural roads that she went on were dreadful. She had already whacked the sump on a dry riverbed, filming the *Living Classroom* series for the Hunters' Association of Zimbabwe, which she co-presented with Kim Damstra.

"Oh, Mister, if the BMW is as splendid as you say, it will handle anything," she pointed out.

During the school holidays I joined her on several film shoots, as a trainee camera woman and general dogsbody. On one such trip, we were on the way home after a long day filming footage for her documentary *Strong Roots*, when she detoured to Ewanrigg Botanical Gardens to get shots of the aloes in bloom. The Ewanrigg River was in flood and further downstream Pattie spotted a group of washerwomen sitting on a rocky outcrop rinsing their laundry in the raging water. It was an ideal shot for her documentary but rather than staggering down to them with her bad hip, she found a slippery footpath for the BMW which slid to a stop a few metres from the river.

With my tripod plugged into soggy soil, I filmed filler shots of the panoramic views while Pattie applied fresh lipstick and put on a large hat to tame her wild, auburn hair. Once presentable, she positioned herself in front of the washerwomen with the flooding river behind and gave Willie the signal to start recording. She began with her usual opening spiel:

"Hello viewers, today we are on the banks of the Ewanrigg River…"

As I zoomed in to get a close-up of the raging water, an ominous shadow rolled into the camera frame. Mister's pride and joy glided majestically past, gathering momentum until it hit a small rock and flipped upside down in the river. The roof caved in on impact, windows exploded, and it was carried off on an angry wave.

"Stop! Stop!" Pattie shouted, the microphone still in her hand.

Willie pressed the pause button and the washerwomen stopped scrubbing their clothes, as per Pattie's instruction.

"Stop!" Pattie shrieked.

The BMW eventually obeyed and crunched to a stop at the weir, prompting a chorus of relief from all witnesses. I remained frozen to the camera, giving chase was pointless and visual evidence would make the explanation to Norman a little easier.

A farmer who had been digging a trench nearby witnessed the incident and drove his digger to the scene. Without saying a word, he jumped out of the driver's seat and ran the gauntlet along the weir attaching a rope around the BMW's upside-down drive shaft. He tied the other end of the rope to the digger bucket and used every inch of its hydraulic power to pull Norman's car sideways through the water to shore. I joined the funeral procession when it reached land and with help from the digger and the slightly astonished looking washerwomen, we pushed the car over onto its wheels which hit the mud with a thud!

While I stood open mouthed with raised eyebrows in

silent vigil, Pattie searched her pockets for the car keys, (for a moment I thought it was to start the engine; it being so superior and all) - but she opened the boot to check if her handbag had survived the swim. When she saw that it was bone dry, she immediately had visions for a new advert and asked Willie to start recording.

"You know like the advert when the Mercedes went over the cliff!" She squealed.

I kept my distance, not wanting any part in the exploitation of a family tragedy and a prolonged colourful explanation to Mister on how his pride and joy had changed shape.

The farmer gave us a lift and we arrived home in dramatic fashion, wet and muddied. Pattie's hat had conveniently flopped over her eyes as she explained to Mister that she had "absolutely left the automatic gearbox in *park*". Norman was relieved that we were unharmed, but the house was quieter than normal for a week or so, and no one dared mention the BMW again. On the upside, Pattie received a lovely reply from BMW's marketing department, re-affirming the fabulous design of the *you know what*. They'd be in touch if they needed any footage in the future and to top it all, *Strong Roots* won an international award.

To make amends, Pattie altered Norman's pre-retirement trip around Europe to include a detour to Germany where he could buy a 190D Mercedes, whose engine, he remarked, was the next big thing. His smile was back again and Lovebug could only use the Mercedes for functions within Harare, excluding the annual church fancy dress competition. The date of which was marked on Pattie's calendar with a fat red circle!

As the fancy dress day loomed, Christianne and I waited with trepidation for Pattie's wondrous creations to appear. Her excitement soon won us over and despite moaning and groaning we usually popped on whatever outfit she had lovingly made. That year, we got away lightly because she was too busy filming to make something up herself and she hired a Chinese dragon costume from the Women's Voluntary Service (WVS) instead. It should've been raised up on poles, but they didn't fit in the Anglia, so Christianne and I ducked underneath wearing bright red stockings and held it up ourselves. Christianne's head popped out between the dragon's jaws and her green eyes guided us around the church stage where she got the dragon to do some interesting Zumba moves. The creature was cumbersome and difficult for the two of us to keep tame, especially when Christianne stepped up the Zumba and blew on a duck call whistle to keep us in rhythm. Pattie had found the whistle in an old box and thought it would give us more character.

"Mum, we're supposed to be a dragon not a duck!" I grumbled.

"Oh, darling, it'll get you noticed,' she replied.

We tired quickly and when the dragon's stomach slumped on the ground, I lost control of its swishing tail and was sent tumbling into the stage wings. We received a rosette for Best Effort, which was not surprising considering the sheer mass of what we had dragged around the stage. Pattie accepted the rosette while we happily tackled the beast back into the boot of the Anglia.

As we got older, it became easier to refuse Pattie's requests to participate in the fancy dress competitions, particularly if I reminded her about the saga of my last compulsory appearance on the church stage. The memory always brought a smile to our faces, and I was sure to over-dramatize the story, reiterating that the incident had left me scarred for life!

On that occasion Pattie found the time in her busy work schedule to dress me up as the scarecrow Worzel Gummidge. She cut a hole in an old beige bedsheet, flung it over my head and tied a tattered leather belt around my waist with a couple of large buttons tacked to the front. To make it look like I was staked out in a field, two broom handles were formed into a cross and the horizontal bar was tied to the back of my arms with a bit of macrame string. The vertical bar was painted to look like grass in a field and once the ends of the sheet were gathered at my wrists, I was stuffed to the brim with straw. Mud was smeared over my face and a curiously shaped homemade bowler hat with more grass painted on it, was plonked on my head. Norman's size 11 veldskoen[14] shoes were taped around my size fours. They flapped around out of control below an enormous pair of work suit trousers that had been found in Norman's workshop and stuffed with more straw. He said that I looked "absolutely splendid," and was ever grateful that his Mercedes had escaped carrying a load "looking like that!".

"You look lovely, darling," said Pattie.

She was dressed up like a typical pirate apart from her slinky knee-high boots which she felt added pizzazz to her outfit. A black patch covered one of her eyes and her eyebrow pencil had to be sharpened twice to colour in her hefty fake moustache and a front tooth. A substantial homemade sword wrapped in kitchen foil swung from her hips and left a trail of destruction behind her.

Swishing it in the air like Blackbeard, she growled at me in her best pirate accent, "heave-ho me hearty, we'll be shark bait if we're late!"

Stuffed with straw and bound to a cross, wearing oversized shoes and a wayward bowler hat, it was difficult to move yet alone pick up the pace. By the time I got to the two-door Anglia, Pattie was anxious to get going but instantly realised that I wasn't going to fit inside. She began emergency readjustments with a brisk de-stuffing of straw to reduce the

---

14. Afrikaans word for walking shoes made of leather or soft rawhide.

size of my girth and squashed the bowler hat further down onto my head. Norman was summoned from his workshop and had to saw off a few centimetres from each end of the broom handles, carefully avoiding the radial arteries in my wrists. Pushing me through the small space between the door and the folded driver's seat they both started to giggle. Bits of my straw rained down on the interior of the car and through the rear-view mirror I could see Pattie stifling her laughter by blowing away bits of straw from her face. She tooted the horn and waved goodbye to Norman who was doubled over laughing in the carpark, waving us off with his wood saw in the air.

A kilometre from church the Anglia spluttered and rolled to a stop on a grassy verge with steam pouring out the engine. Pattie tried to get help by waving down cars while I extracted myself with difficulty to avoid my crispy innards possibly catching fire for whatever reason. Most of the cars sped up going past us, others swerved away from a flustered, black toothed, sword wielding pirate and a beady looking scarecrow searching for places to hide.

"You could walk ahead, it's not far darling." Pattie shouted from the road.

I didn't respond but she leapt onto the front seat when a brave-hearted man driving a pickup truck came to our rescue. I only agreed to get into the back if my bowler hat was pushed right down over my nose to avoid eye contact with rubbernecking road users. We made a dramatic late entrance and while I remained tied to my homemade cross in a church hall, Pattie happily received the rosette for third place on my behalf. She descended the steps of the church stage waving her sword and the rosette in the air like she had just won an Oscar.

Norman was still laughing when he came to collect us and

explained how he'd traced our route by following wayward bits of my straw like Hansel and Gretel all the way along Stonechat Lane to St Gerard's Church. He was delighted that the ordeal saw the demise of the Ford Anglia and discussed buying Lovebug a car that was more suitable for her work and for carrying scarecrows or dragons where necessary but made sure my entire costume was dumped in the church bins before taking us home in his Mercedes.

****

16

I turned off my laptop when Mistake arrived to take us to the Ume Junior School. He was holding chunks of cinnamon soap in both hands and explained that he had split the axe block trying to chop the soap up into more manageable pieces, which didn't surprise me in the least. Wonder placed them on a paper towel so as not to stain his pantry shelves and suggested that we get going if we wanted to meet Debbie and Hans at the school by 7am.

Mike and Witness were excited to meet a teacher from a high-profile school in Harare. Strutting around Jules, they explained that they had 60 pupils aged between 6 and 11 who were split into three classes. Jules jabbed me in the ribs when Witness confirmed that they were one teacher short, and lessons were currently juggled between classrooms.

At 7.15am sharp, Mike rang the school bell enthusiastically and 60 bright-eyed children marched into their classrooms in single file, squeezing together onto wooden benches neatly spaced in rows. Hans had recently made the benches and had replaced the shade cloth walls with homemade breeze block bricks. Pupils and teachers alike beamed with pride at their new facilities.

We followed Mike into the first classroom, where he scrawled a maths sum on the board. The children copied it into exercise books on their laps, but lost concentration when Jules walked the rows examining their work. They'd never seen a female teacher before; men were usually the educated ones in their culture.

"How many girls are at the school?" Jules enquired.

"Three," Mike confirmed.

They were huddled together on their own bench in the next classroom, breaking the social norm. Hope beamed from their eyes when Jules walked up to them and said good morning. One little girl took her hand as we moved to the third classroom, shadowed by 40 inquisitive children from the first two classes. We learned from Mike and Witness that they didn't have an up-to-date curriculum or enough exercise books, pencils and rulers. Jules planned to rectify that immediately.

There were three swings in the dusty playground, the seats were worn thin by 60 children vying for a turn every break time. Hans planned to build them a jungle gym and had started planting a lawn to reduce the heat and dust. Debbie had prepared beds for a new garden and was explaining the potential for arts and crafts classes when a massive baboon leapt out of a rubbish pit with half a pumpkin under its arm. Hans walked me over to the pit and explained that it was once a swimming pool. If we could raise the funds to get it repaired, I could teach swimming. There was so much to do!

We returned to the lodge hot and dusty and flopped into the swimming pool to cool off. Bursting with excitement, plans for a new life whirled around in our heads.

"I'd have to update my lifesavers certificate to teach swimming again and we could bring pool paint to the Ume on the Transporter," I suggested.

"We could revamp the school and paint the breeze blocks in an environmentally friendly colour, the swings too" Jules added.

While we were discussing various colour palettes, the swimming pool waterfall started to splutter. Fancying myself as a fledgling pool guru, I assumed that the skimmer basket needed to be emptied of leaves and twigs but sent the lid flying when two claws reached out and touched my hand. Re-armed with the leaf scoop, which Mistake had since reattached with wire, I peered inside the bowl and saw something yellow swirling at the bottom. For a minute I thought that the Tsanga Nyoka had returned and had come to a nasty end.

Jules rushed to turn off the pool pump and once the water had settled, we could see that a leguaan[15] was trapped by its tongue in the filter pipe joint. Every few minutes it used its powerful tail to propel to the surface and gulp for air, stretching its trapped tongue further and further each time. We had to act fast.

"Do leguaans bite?" I asked.

"Hurry, Lissie, please," Jules pushed me towards it.

I was reluctant to put my hand into such a confined space, but the poor creature was struggling. When it appeared on the surface again, I used a forked twig to pin its head and what looked like teeth to one side and slipped my other hand into the bowl to release the clamp. The leguaan wriggled free and swam desperately through the filter suction hole and into the basin of the swimming pool. Its tongue had been stretched out of proportion and flowed alongside the entire length of its body.

We watched with delight as the lizard surfaced for air in the deep end and swam in small circles catching its breath. Seconds later it rolled onto its back and sank back to the bottom!

Jules latched onto the pool scoop slapping the water in a frenzied attempt to bring the leguaan back to the surface. The leaf scoop came loose again and both the net and the leguaan were hanging on by a thread when she used Mistake's grass broom to rescue them both from the depths. The creature

---

15. A large African monitor lizard

looked dead when she shook it out onto the lawn, but after taking a moment to recover it scurried through the makeshift fence into the budding strelitzias, dragging its long pink tongue behind. Jules immediately put out a saucer of milk to aid its recovery. I wasn't sure if leguaans drank milk, or how it was supposed to lap from a saucer with an overstretched tongue, but I didn't air my thoughts.

The rumble of Hans' motorbike diverted our attention away from the leguaan and we thought that an impromptu fishing session was on the cards. After leaning his bike against a tree, Hans walked towards us looking flustered and announced that there was a major breakdown in the factory. He needed to go to Harare at first light to collect spares and Debbie would go with him to visit her children. Instead of waiting for our transfer in two days' time, he suggested that we catch a lift in their boat, which was a great idea. The heat was getting a bit much and besides, if all went to plan, Jules and I would be back in the Ume soon.

We had an early evening booze cruise around Bird Island where another big tiger fish was waiting to be caught on our return. The manager of the crocodile farm joined us for a farewell fish pie dinner and after listening to our plans for the school, he burst our bubble in seconds.

"There will be trouble with the upcoming Presidential elections, it will not be safe for you here."

The Ume area was an opposition stronghold and political violence was likely during the run-up. He had already planned to send Debbie away for the duration.

We packed our suitcases in silence and tore the fishing rods apart. I threw them both into the empty tin trunk and I slammed down the lid. The left-over groceries were distributed out to Mistake and Wonder, and the only items left in the pantry were a carton of long-life milk for the leguaan and chunks of cinnamon soap for anyone who fancied a carbolic pink rinse. After a quick recce around the lodge for any forgotten belongings, we went to bed devastated.

Edith was bleating for her treats early the next morning. As I emptied the last of the maputi onto the lawn Gertrude head-butted Shawn and Stewart out the way and took a few pieces from my hand. I tried to stroke her to say goodbye, but she would have none of it and sashayed to the bottom of the garden. Dressed in his chef's whites, Wonder bowed his head and put out his hand to say goodbye.

"God bless you and good luck with your book," he smiled.

"Thanks for everything Wonder; I'll send you a copy when it's printed."

Mistake loaded the tin trunk onto the wheelbarrow and after topping up the leguaan's milk, we followed him through the perimeter gate, dragging our feet down the path to the harbour. I had a quick look for the angry buffalo bull in the Jesse bush and wondered whether the story had been a ruse as we hadn't seen him once or perhaps, he was the unfortunate one eaten by the lions on our first night.

Ambling along the wooden jetty I took in the last sights and smells of the harbour and stepped onto Hans' boat with ease. Mistake passed over my laptop with Pattie's bag of lost treasures attached and I put out my hand to say goodbye.

"You're welcome," he smiled.

"I'll get Hans a new leaf scoop in Harare and post your football photographs. Look after our sheep, Mistake, and don't forget to change your name when you turn 21."

It was a bright still day. The shoreline was void of elephants, but the hippos snorted goodbye, or good riddance. Nyami Nyami was resting up in the coolness of the deep water and the Lake was like glass. I watched the Ume Conservancy shrink into the Matusadona Mountains and eventually disappear. The crossing back to Kariba took an hour and a half; I wished desperately that it had taken longer.

****

17

Our journey back from the Ume was as quiet as the one up there, but for different reasons. Plans for a new life across the Lake had collapsed and memories of Pattie were waiting for us at home. We were in no rush to return until the electric gate opened and Hildah, Scruffy, Muffin and both the cats stampeded the car to greet us.

"God is there!" Hildah shouted, as the gate closed.

"Stop it Scruffy," she called, "it's me, Hildah."

He couldn't care less who she was, barking and bumping his way around her ankles to be the first to meet me in the car park.

In our absence the house had returned to normal, and the sound of Pattie's crutches no longer ticked down the passageway, but we tiptoed to our room out of habit anyway.

After a detailed report on home affairs from Hildah, I phoned Christianne for the full update on Pattie. The clear connection and comfortable seat were a dull improvement on the anthill phone booth on the edge of the Ume River, but it was good to speak to her and get all the news.

Vicki was my next call, she had just got back from England and said that her prayer book had come in handy on the flight, but offered no more detail than that, knowing it wouldn't do any good.

I phoned the respite home, and the manager kept me on hold while he tracked Pattie down through the corridors. The image vivid in my mind as the sound of her ticking crutches grew louder.

"Hello, Mum, it's me, Lissie." I choked. She didn't respond.

"Mum, are you there?"

"Help, help!" she sobbed.

"What's the matter, Mum, are you alright?" I pleaded.

She laughed and said something incomprehensible.

"Christianne says your room is lovely," I interrupted.

"No!" she guffawed.

Scruffy barked at Hildah again and I shouted at them both to keep quiet; the conversation was hard enough without added noise.

"Scruffy is being naughty with Hildah, Mum. He misses you," I said, stupidly.

"Yes," she whimpered.

I changed the subject, asking more daft questions about the home, which I knew she couldn't answer. Christianne had sent pictures of the bedsit, which looked lovely and was filled with family photographs and familiar belongings.

"Come!" she trembled.

"Soon, Mum, soon." I said, upbeat.

"Don't be long, darling," she replied.

"I won't, Mum. Is that a new friend near you?" I asked, hearing another voice.

"OK, darling. Love you."

"I love you too, Mum."

Those words came easily for Pattie; they always had, and her instinct seemed to know that I needed to hear it. But she dropped the cordless phone without saying goodbye and it didn't ring off. My tears welled as the sound of her crutches grew fainter and someone started shouting at her.

"Come on then, come on!"

"I can't, I can't!" Pattie screamed.

A carer interrupted them and asked if everything was alright, and my imagination exploded with dreadful images.

"Mum, are you alright? Hello, hello is anyone there?" I yelled down the receiver.

"Help! I can't!" I heard again.

"Will someone help her!" I screamed.

It sounded like my mother was being dragged down the corridor by her hair. I couldn't listen any further and rang off, speed dialling Christianne's number.

"Oh, that's Betty," she said calmly.

My sister had rapidly developed relationships with all the staff and knew most of the 43 residents by name. Betty's Alzheimer's was at the same stage as Pattie, and they roamed the corridors together.

As the months went by Christianne and I realised that we would have to break my promise to our mother. Neither of us could cope with her illness and with 24-hour care Pattie was in the right place. She had a lovely room, great food and lots of company. It was the hardest decision to apply for her permanent residency in the home, but the right one.

As her illness progressed, she started to forget that she needed crutches to walk, especially when she got out of bed in the morning. After the first fall she needed three stitches above her eye and lost a front tooth in the second fall. Without the front tooth, her dentures no longer fitted which made her look worse, especially because she still smiled so much. I was absolutely fuming, she hadn't fallen once with me, but her illness was degenerative and who was I to judge from 12 000 kilometres away. How do you remind an Alzheimer's sufferer to use crutches to get around? How do you stop them from walking the passageways non-stop? More drugs or a straitjacket? For God's sake, this is my mother we are talking about! One small consolation was that as her brain died, she would feel less pain and would soon forget how to walk altogether. In the meantime, she was put into a hospital bed with side rails and could only get out if someone else released the plunger to lower the rails.

I made the decision only to phone the home when Christianne was there visiting. Having her describe to me what was going on allayed my fears and calmed my imagination. I had to psych myself up to speak each time, but my spirits always lifted when I heard my mother's voice and hung on to every comprehensible word she said.

"Hello, my darling!" she replied once in a jolly tone.

"I love you, Mum."

"I love you, my treasure," she sobbed, using the term of endearment from her father.

Christianne said I shouldn't get upset when Pattie cried. They were mostly dry tears and a form of recognition; would I know the difference if they were real? I started to pray again, mostly for one thing – that the carers would be kind to my mother.

Christmas came and went and Christianne attended a joyous carol service watching 43 people at varying levels of the disease banging on objects and trying to sing *"Rudolph the Red-nosed Reindeer"*. Pattie continued weekly flower arranging classes and did nothing other than snip off the buds with plastic scissors.

Four months after I'd sent her away, she became a permanent resident of the home. Rooms were in demand and difficult to get, so it was wonderful news for the new year, I suppose. I hadn't felt like doing any writing since leaving the Ume River and needed to get myself together and finish my mother's story. I'd hoped to present the book to her sooner rather than later, but she wouldn't know what day it was anyway.

****

18

When I got my driver's licence at 16 years old, Pattie and Norman immediately bought me a second-hand car. Having my own wheels saved them endless hours taxiing me to and from school, horse riding lessons, afternoon sports and club hockey training in the evenings. From the outside, my green Vauxhall Deluxe looked like it had rolled out of an army surplus store, but I felt like a queen on the inside perched on a large cushion on top of green leather seats just so I could see over the enormous wooden steering wheel. The interior had oak trimmings and a drinks bar with backseat trays and cup holders. An exhausted cassette player frequently blasted out favourite songs from UB40, Bananarama, Spandau Ballet and the Eurythmics. Its bouncy seats carried many friends who, like me, explored the joys of adolescent freedom on many trips to the drive-in cinema.

Before I was let loose on the roads, Norman insisted on taking me on a test drive where he asked me to wind down the window and listen to the engine.

"Can you hear the whine in the differential, Liza?' he asked, using the name he liked to call me.

He thought it a breakthrough when I did hear something, I think! I couldn't care what the noise was, so long as it got me to horse-riding lessons, hockey training and clandestine meetings with my first boyfriend, Jeff.

I spent most school holidays at the riding stables with fellow riders, Simon, Gregg, and Julie (not to be confused with Jules). They owned their horses, but I had a car, and the combination was teenage bliss. When my horse-riding skills improved enough Pattie and Norman bought me a pony and Julie and I started to compete in Pony Club trials and were inseparable.

Pattie had just two house-rules for her teenage daughters: Be home by curfew and be up in time for Sunday morning's 7am Mass. Rules that I found difficult to keep with such a hectic social and sporting calendar. I was the youngest and smallest in the League hockey team. Jenny, the captain, and Linda, the goalkeeper, took me under their wing and pushed me all the way to represent my country and became lifelong friends. I frequently stayed late at Old Hararians Sports Club after training when my Vauxhall freewheeled into the driveway at home, mostly undetected, late at night. If the kettle was still warm when I got home, Pattie would be awake, and I should have a worthy explanation for my tardiness at the ready.

Attending Sunday Mass at 7am together as a family was important to Pattie and I mostly dragged myself to it, compos mentis or not.

"You can make your own decision about church when you're 18!' She asserted.

She would say an extra prayer for my tired red eyes, as I read the Sacraments out loud at an ungodly hour in the morning. I couldn't wait to come of age when I would neither get up early nor witness my mother's sadness, each time I left her behind at the pew to receive Holy communion. Norman found the Catholic service lengthy but enjoyed belting out the protracted hymns, ensuring that I suffered every moment of the night's gallivanting.

During the hockey season, I was allowed to leave church early to get to the field in time for the Sunday league games.

Pattie never failed to arrive after Mass, armed with her new video camera to capture me in action. Norman was never without two red promotional cushions that Lovebug had designed and produced in their hundreds for the St George's College Centenary celebration. They were perfect padding for Pattie's bad hip on the wooden spectators' benches, but she never sat for long before circling the hockey field with her camera, in search of me.

"Hello, darling," she whispered, popping out from behind the goal after a short corner.

The referee frequently had to stop play and move her further away from the action. Her limp and sudden bursts of enthusiasm made the camera unsteady which mostly captured snippets of body parts and tops of heads. Unsuspecting visitors to our home were often forced to watch each frame, where she openly admitted that the filming should be left to her cameraman, Willie, but it didn't stop her from filming the next game.

Wherever she was, the "lady from Sunday television" drew an admiring crowd. Pattie always took the time to chat with them and occasionally signed autographs while Norman read his newspapers and caught up on the latest cricket news.

When Julie and I started to compete in three-phase (cross country, show jumping and dressage), Pattie learnt to tow a horse box with her second-hand Toyota truck that had replaced the Anglia. She drove us around the country, camping on the farms where the competitions were being held. Norman thought camping was a "ghastly" idea and stayed behind, but Pattie loved the adventure of visiting new places and meeting new people. Always looking out for new storylines for the next documentary.

On one occasion, she safely negotiated towing the horsebox through heavy traffic on the Mutare Road and drove us to Larkhill Farm in Marondera, an hour outside

Harare. We found a campsite under Msasa trees and positioned the truck and horsebox in a semi-circle around a stone braai and picnic table. Julie and I slept in the horsebox and Pattie slept on a mattress under the truck canopy with a duvet, continental pillows, and a night light for reading. It was "better than a hotel," she said, but she struggled to get out of it in the morning. Stoking the morning fire, her joy of being in the bush was obvious and her rendition of *'Morning Has Broken'* often woke the campsite. Sleepy-eyed competitors emerged from their tents to join her at the campfire where a giant black kettle simmered with morning tea next to an ancient tin filled with ginger biscuits.

Before the cross country started, she canvassed the course to find the best spots to film me in action. My pony, Tosca, mostly thought it unnecessary to jump over obstacles when she could go around them, particularly when a strange woman wearing an enormous bush hat, popped out from behind the bushes with a video camera instructing her to jump to the moon!

The dressage competition started at 8am on Sunday and with it came every possibility of missing Mass. However, Pattie had received intelligence that a rural church a few kilometres down the road, offered a Shona service at six-thirty in the morning. Timing would be tight for the start of the competition and worshipping in another language, tricky, but not impossible.

The moon was still up when she brought a cup of tea and bowl of porridge to the horsebox and suggested we dress in our riding gear to save time. The quiet church shook from its stone foundation when we roared to a halt in tall grass near the entrance, having come down a footpath of some sort! Pattie burst onto the scene waving hello and calling a group of children who were playing football to gather under a Msasa tree for a photograph.

By the time we got into the church, it was full, but Pattie spotted a few vacant seats in the middle aisle and squeezed along the pew, trying not to concuss worshippers with her video camera. All eyes were on us, particularly on Julie and me. Most had never seen jodhpurs and knee-high riding boots with spurs. Our hair was in nets and our Pony Club neckties and black jackets added to their curiosity.

As the opening hymn began, drums, mbiras[16], and rattles shook into rhythm along our bench, rejoicing the Lord and celebrating the fact that we had just unwittingly joined the choir!

"Isn't this lovely?" Pattie said, humming the Shona tune.

I understood some of what was being sung, thanks to the teachings of Mr Patsanza, and felt anonymous in the beautiful sounds until it was time to go up and receive Holy Communion. Julie and I left Pattie at the pew and marched down the aisle towards the priest, breaking the reverence with a quartet of horse spurs clattering on the stone floor, like the cavalry had just arrived.

After Mass, Pattie thanked the priest for the lovely service and received a list of the church needs to add to her own parish notices. Filming an appreciative crowd, she found it difficult to get away especially after her budding film stars discovered the joys of instant replay on her camera. She eventually tooted the horn and waved goodbye to her newfound friends, and we raced back to Larkhill just in time for the competition.

To complete the dressage course, I trotted Tosca down the centre line and was about to come to a halt and salute the judges when a groom dropped a metal bucket nearby. Having been spooked all weekend Tosca had enough. She

---

16. A traditional Shona musical instrument consisting of a wooden board with metal tines.

shied then reared, knocking my hard hat off which pulled my hair net down over my eyes. When the hard hat hit the ground, she bolted over the arena fence, clipping the judges' umbrella on the way out.

"That's Pattie's daughter," I heard them say as we disappeared out of sight.

My hair net was found in a bush some distance away from the arena and despite my disqualification, a photograph of my pony and me appeared on the back page of *The Herald* newspaper the following week. Pattie had slipped it into a promotional advert announcing an upcoming documentary on the history of the Horse Society in Zimbabwe. Thankfully the photograph had been taken before Tosca had bolted!

During the making of the documentary, Pattie decided that my camera work had improved enough for me to film her interview with Mrs WC, the current Chairlady of the Horse Society. She was a real character and I found it difficult to keep my composure as she recalled pertinent bits of its history:

"Well, you see, Pattie, in 1920-something, the first cross country in Rhodesia was held and I won it, ha ha ha. In 1924, I won it again, ha, ha, ha. I did not win it in 1925 because I was preggers!"

Pattie thought she was fabulous, as was her groom, who she thought had the incredible name of Pass-me-a-badza[17].

"So, tell me, Mr Pass-me-a-badza, when did you start working for Mrs WC?" Pattie enquired, with a perfectly straight face.

"You're not putting that on television, Mum?" I asked with tears of laughter rolling down my cheeks.

"Oh, darling, I think it's lovely," she squealed.

****

---

17. A tool used for digging with a flat iron blade attached to a wooden handle.

19

Christianne left school after her GCSEs to study beauty therapy at the Harare Polytechnic. Her presence at home was ghostly, as she discovered the joys of first loves and nightclubs with her childhood friends Annie and Laurie, who were all developing into beautiful young ladies. I left the Dominican Convent a year later and enrolled at Chisipite Senior School. In contrast to my sister, I was a tomboy, who was barely seen out of jodhpurs and tracksuits, which Pattie felt needed to change. She had just graduated from a Silhouette Studio over-fifties modelling course and "becoming a young lady" started to dominate conversations at the dinner table. Especially as the date approached for the New Year's Eve party at the Harare Men's Social Club, where Norman was an avid member.

Pattie had recently agreed to do the PR for the Club and had become its first female associate member, sending rumbles down the corridors of this revered bastion of masculinity. She had plans to become a full member and hoped to curve-ball some sunshine onto its walls, which were presently plastered with drab pictures of past presidents and colonial buildings. Norman looked forward to the party and loved the formality of lavish tables with a silver service presented by white-gloved, penguin-suited waiters.

In preparation for the event, Pattie and Julie's mother, Beverley, connived to book us on a teenage grooming course. Julie and I spent a hideous week learning to groom ourselves instead of our horses. To crown our glory, Norman and

Julie's grandmother, Lena, decided to give us dancing lessons on the waltz and the quickstep.

The day before the party, Christianne used all her beauty therapy training to make sure every unnecessary hair was removed from our bodies with hot wax, which wasn't a pleasant experience. Our brows were plucked, nails painted, and makeup lathered on. Julie and I squeezed into our new shimmering, shapely dresses and formidable court shoes and incredibly looked just the part on the night.

The lengthy formal occasion was exhausting, I gave up trying to choose the correct utensils early and was relieved when the cut glass dessert bowls clattered away on trolleys at the end of the meal. As the music began to play Norman took Lovebug to the floor for the first dance. She was dressed in a dazzling green sequined ball gown, and he was wearing a crisp white shirt with a dickie tie underneath a jet-black tuxedo suit. They looked magnificent as he held her tightly, steadying her bad leg during a slow waltz. Before the start of the next song, he proudly walked her back to the table and put out his hand to me. Counting 1-2-3 under my breath, we got into the rhythm of another civilized waltz. Heads turned as my court shoes clacked around the parquet flooring of the Cecil John Rhodes Hall conquering a few death-defying spins and Norman couldn't have been prouder.

The atmosphere was cordial and dull until several glasses of wine took effect on two teenagers and our favourite practice song, *Boogie Woogie Bugle Boy*, erupted from the crackly speakers. Julie and I took our positions as we would have done in practice sessions and quickstepped around the floor, diverting onto the carpet and around a few startled diners to ask the barman to turn the music up. Eyes from the portraits of past presidents followed two women on the dance floor and watched a hundred years of protocol shatter. Pattie giggled at our audacity, but on the stroke of 12, Norman gave Lovebug the first kiss and whisked us away before we created any further excitement. Once we were in the car, he commented that our quickstep was satisfactory, but we needed more sharpness in our footwork on the quarter turn to the right!

Within a few years of gaining independence, cracks began to appear in the Zimbabwean economy. An exodus of skilled workers flowed through border posts, just as it had done in Malawi. Government expenditure tripled to bolster the economic inequality of the Smith Regime, and the Zimbabwe dollar devalued; this, together with a deficit in the budget, created a critical shortage of foreign currency. The Country could still feed itself but imported all its fuel. The lack of foreign currency led to fuel shortages and rationing was introduced.

Fuel usage at home was restricted to Pattie's work or charity needs and Norman's weekly trip to Ruwa Golf Club or the Harare Men's Club Friday lunches. My fuel-guzzling Vauxhall was immediately parked, and I used a bicycle or a horse to get around and experienced a few hair-raising journeys on the handlebars of Jeff's bicycle! I wonder what *Charles Letts* would have to say about that! Julie and I often joined the fuel queues at Helensvale garage on horseback with jerry cans strapped to the saddles. Pattie thought it was a marvellous solution saving her endless wasted hours in queues.

Once a week I caught a lift with her to the riding stables where she'd started volunteering for the Riding for the Disabled. Despite her hip, she managed several slow walks around the arena with a blind four-year-old child in the saddle. The little girl used to run towards Pattie's voice with her arms outstretched. The need for volunteers and riding hats were added to the church notices. Pattie's sister Margaret volunteered as did Vicki's mother, Delia, who'd just moved to Harare from Redcliffe in the Midlands, and it was where they first met.

At one point, fuel was so short that I rode Tosca 24 kilometers to school and back. The Deputy Headmaster kept horses on a plot nearby and he allowed me to leave my pony there while I was in class. To comply with school uniform regulations Pattie sewed a thick elastic strap to my basher to keep it on my head while on horseback. After a quick cup of tea and a prayer to St Christopher she watched me galloping blissfully into the rising sun along Crowhill Road with a satchel on my back.

Pattie's work schedule remained full despite the fuel crisis, but her hip was getting worse, and she was struggling to get around. The orthopaedic consultant confirmed that she needed a second hip replacement on the same side.

"Can you make me six foot, blonde and blue-eyed while you're doing it?" she cackled with him.

With Norman's love and support, Christianne and I felt far less vulnerable this time around. The new hip joint promised miracles, but her leg didn't work properly again. For the first time, she appeared on television using crutches. Smiling into the camera with a microphone in her hand and limping over hills, through caves and down mines showed viewers that it was alright to be different and that disability didn't mean inability.

****

20

After 35 years as Managing Director of Triple Jay Engineering, Norman retired in the confidence that his meticulously planned pension would comfortably fund his golden years. With time on his hands, he rebuilt the "dreadful" cottage at the bottom of the garden and replaced the French doors at the front of the main house with an elevated bay window. It was the perfect spot for Pattie to admire her view and find inspiration for her scriptwriting. Below the bay window, a padded, carpeted sunken TV lounge was easily converted into a comfortable dormitory for our friends to collapse onto after a night on the town. The white granite sideboard that he erected in the dining room was a masterpiece and so solid that we knew to take shelter under it, if ever there was an earthquake! He couldn't find a way to fix the narrow, crooked passageway to the bedrooms which remained a source of irritation to his engineering mind.

The house repairs came to a grinding halt every Friday when he downed tools and burnt rubber to attend a weekly lunch at the Harare Men's Social Club. It was a place where he could discuss all sorts of manly matters and the three-course meal was usually followed by a hotly contested game of billiards. He was always home by six o' clock sharp and never without a bunch of flowers for Lovebug. The shape of the bouquet that arrived home depended entirely on the number of glasses of wine he'd had over lunch, but they always brought a smile to Pattie's face. One bunch of roses were at right angles having been accidentally slammed in the car door. He presented them to her with tears of laughter running down his face and they both ended up in bits as he explained what had happened. Pattie was dreadful at flower arranging anyway and was relieved not to have to struggle with the flowers that week!

"They look beautiful just as they are, Mister," she giggled, plonking them in a vase.

My Gran, Veronica, died that year. She was 90 years old. It was a good age, but we thought she would live forever, and our family was devasted. Since moving to Chisipite Senior School I'd stopped spending afternoons with her, and the fuel shortages restricted visits. The last time we were together, she showed off her certificate of appreciation from St John's Ambulance for 70 years' service as a street collector. Her funeral at the Harare Catholic Cathedral overflowed with schoolgirls and "have you told your mother how much you love her today?" dominated conversations. As her coffin left the church, I knew the school block would never be the same but felt sure St Peter would accept the large collection of *green stamps* that she had accumulated during her long life.

I blossomed at Chisipite School and befriended two other newbies: Aggie, who wanted to become a professional game guide and could strip down a weapon in seconds, and Bella, who wore crazy catsuits and aspired to be a paediatric nurse. Julie went on to Arundel Senior School and had plans to study Journalism. My friends were strong, determined women who made me want to achieve more.

When they stayed the night, we spent hours around the dinner table with Norman, spinning bottles of wine around the lazy Susan, debating issues, telling jokes, and groaning when he brought up an engineering topic. The evening typically ended with sing-a-longs and Norman's rendition of his Latin school song which frequently woke the rest of the house. Watching him mesmerise my friends with *"Quotquot annos, quotquot menses"* I realised he had become the father I never had.

I ultimately parted with my pony, Tosca, but not before Pattie pushed us into participating in our final charity fancy dress competition for the Pony Club. Christianne's Mini Cooper was converted into a *Chariot of Fire* for the occasion. It was wrapped completely in brown paper to conceal its identity with two gigantic polystyrene wings of fire glued to each side. Julie sat on the roof like a chariot driver and held onto pseudo reigns attached to three horses with Simon, Gregg and me on top of each of them, holding plastic torches of fire. Pattie drove the car blind, but Julie guided her into the arena and around the jumps by tapping signals for left and right on the roof. As the judges handed out our rosette for third place, Pattie tooted the horn and her hand burst through the brown wrapping paper into the air.

"Don't forget mine!" she shrieked.

We found Tosca a stress-free home with Margaret and a magnificent three-quarter horse, classified as a Junior A grade showjumper, replaced her. Highly Explosive was aptly named and much more experienced than me. As it happened, our first show jumping competition was the biggest in the country. Due to the fuel shortages, Pattie couldn't tow the horse box to site, so Julie and I rode the horses 25 kilometres to the showgrounds the day before.

Thousands of people converged at the Harare Easter Show to view new products and equipment and watch farmers parade prize farm stock. Children of all ages queued for rides at Luna Park, the country's only amusement fairground. The home industries hall was packed with incredible cakes, jams, needlework, and knitwear submitted by housewives vying to be crowned champions. Margaret's tomato jam had won first prize and a few of our art pieces submitted by Maureen hung on the walls with commendations.

The Easter Show ended with the Grand Prix show jumping event in Glamis Arena, where Highly Explosive wanted to jump to the moon, and I quivered at the ridiculous size of the jumps. With a packed grandstand, his nostrils flared, and haunches pinched as we approached the towering triple jump.

"Go Lissie!" Pattie waved from the VIP section of the stand.

She had just completed the production of a 26-six-week series for the cattle industry of Zimbabwe called *Cattle Call*. Next to her in the stand was a group of white jacketed sunburnt farmers who she'd dragged along to watch me dig my spur in too early, poorly timing Highly Explosive's stride. He flew over the first jump, plopped over the second and screeched to a halt on the third – sending me flying into the crossbar.

"Go Lissie!" echoed from the stands.

Pattie had mislaid her glasses and couldn't see that the horse cantering around the arena was minus her daughter, whose hand had gone up to retire from the ground. I lost my nerve from that moment on and Highly Explosive was sold to a more deserving rider, ending my horse-riding years. But bottles of wine whirled around on the lazy Susan when I passed my A Levels, turned 18 and stopped going to seven o' clock morning Mass. Pattie never gave up trying to change my mind on the last point.

Norman replaced my Vauxhall Deluxe with a more fuel-efficient Datsun 120Y, which took Aggie and me to Kariba for a six-day canoeing safari down the Zambezi River to the Mozambique border. Paddling 120 kilometres to Kanyemba gave Aggie the exposure to the bush before her game guide exams and gave me the time to decide whether to accept an invitation to play hockey in America. On the second day of the trip, a hippo attacked our canoe. As it reared and charged,

Aggie stood up, shouting and beating the water with her oar, while I paddled in reverse frantically trying to get our canoe away. The hippo almost had us on several occasions and was so close that we could smell its foul breath before it porpoise dived underwater and surfaced again with its mouth open. The attack carried on for twenty minutes until we reached deeper water and it eventually tired and returned to its pod. From that moment on, I was extremely wary around hippos.

By the end of the year, Julie and Bella left for university in South Africa and Aggie left for the bush. Two knee injuries and months in full casts ended my hockey career. With plans for my future in tatters, I took a gap year and joined Pattie at PIC films. For a time, both of us were on crutches which made introductions to new clients interesting!

****

21

I was off my crutches by the time John Pile and the Conservation Trust commissioned PIC Films to make a new documentary on the endangered black rhinoceros. Willie sent Ian Jackson along as his substitute cameraman and with me now in the team, we couldn't fit three adults into Pattie's single cab truck. Norman's Mercedes was the only other option.

Clem Coetsee's Rhino camp was based at Ruckomechi in Mana Pools National Park. The roads were ghastly, but Pattie was careful, determined to avoid having to report another car incident to Mister. We held our breath crossing the flooded Ruckomechi River one-way bridge and arrived at the camp late in the afternoon, without having lost a single Mercedes part.

Clem's welcome was warm but brief. He saw most visitors as a necessary intrusion to raise awareness and funds for the capture and relocation of the last 1000 black rhinos left in the wild. His wife, Emily, handled the camp induction and most of the social interaction, leaving Clem to get on with his job.

Her first instruction was for us to put anything made of leather back inside the car to avoid attracting hyenas to the tents during the night. She then showed us the operations tent which was erected in the shade of mopane trees and centred around an enormous campfire. It was Clem's domain and the beating heart of the operation which held tools, radios, veterinary medicine, guns, ammunition, and tinned food stocks. Their sleeping tent was next door and several metres to the left was the camp toilet which was strategically placed under a single mopane tree. Inside its flimsily thatched walls was a large wooden box with a hole cut out in the centre and positioned directly over another hole that was dug deep into the ground, known as a "long drop" for obvious reasons. A loo roll spun around a sturdy nail that was hammered into the tree trunk at just the right height. Thatched circular walls saved the need for a door and the lack of a roof made for good ventilation. Leaves from the mopane tree branches above provided ample shade and dappled light. Although it looked basic Emily assured us that it was totally functional but warned us to check the wooden box for snakes before we went about our business! Our sleeping tent was ten meters from the toilet. It was large enough to fit a battalion and empty apart from two canvas camp beds right at the entrance. Ian had an equally large tent next door.

Emily offered for us to have a bath before dinner if we wanted, but we would need to hurry due to the failing light. After a quick scrummage for our toiletries, Pattie and I followed her down a stony path to the edge of the Ruckomechi River. Tucked behind a half-moon thatched wall sat an enormous sparkling white enamel bath with a large mirror nailed to a tree. She smiled at our surprised look and said that it was her only prerequisite to living in the bush and Clem moved it to every new camp they made. After a demonstration on how to crank down a colossal chunk of soap that dangled high out of reach from hyenas, she left us to take turns to soak. River water had been plumbed into a large drum and warmed by the African sun. It carried enough heat to make the bath luxurious, with incredible views.

After lathering on mosquito repellent, we gathered around

the campfire after our bath and ate mouth-watering impala[18] stew from bowls on our laps. While stoking the campfire, Clem pointed out the sounds of lions and hyenas on the hunt and asked Emily to step in when Pattie enquired about his background. We learnt that he'd joined National Parks at the age of 15 and was an original member of Operation Noah which rescued 6000 wild animals from the rising water of the Zambezi River when Kariba Dam was built. The operation took place between 1958-1964 and Clem had rescued every type of creature from porcupines to birds, snakes, leopards, lions, antelopes, rhinos and elephants. Clem was a shy man of few words who avoided the limelight and disliked taking any credit for himself. He had a toughness earned from years of experience in the bush, but his eyes lit up when I mentioned his daughter, Beth, with whom I'd played hockey, and he chuckled when I recalled a few of our escapades together.

When Emily handed out strong tea in tin cups, Clem started to lock down the camp and the evening ended promptly at 7.30. With a leather rifle case slung over his shoulder, he escorted us to our tent and told us not to go outside alone during the night. He wished us good night, marched back to the operations tent and turned off every light!

Using torch light, Pattie and I moved our camp beds away from the entrance, which somehow felt safer. I pulled the front flap down, pinched the snap fasteners firmly together, knotted the tie backs and placed a few loose bricks along the bottom flap for added security.

Pattie fell asleep easily, but I lay awake for ages listening to the tree frogs and night apes, wishing I hadn't had that last cup of tea and hoping the urge for the loo would pass. I could hear something scratching outside and dozed off wondering

---

18. A medium sized antelope.

if hyenas were chewing through the Mercedes tyres to get at Pattie's leather handbag. Another handbag incident in one of Mister's cars would be an interesting story. I woke up a short while later, bursting.

"Mum, can you wake up, I need to go!"

She sat upright immediately, fumbling for her torch, fighting with the mosquito net like an upturned beetle.

"Can you keep watch?" I giggled.

"Only if you pull me up!" She laughed.

The canvas camp bed was low, and I had to give her a good yank to get her upright. When I snorted, we became hysterical and by the time the snaps and ties were undone on the front flap I ran blindly out into the night.

Pattie kept watch from the safety of the tent: I could see her torch light following the treeline against the night sky. She was searching everywhere other than in my direction, where an elephant had brushed up against the flimsy toilet wall and I'd frozen in fear, mid-flow. Its trunk snaked over the thatch reaching for branches, scattering leaves around my throne. When it started to relieve itself, I couldn't hold mine any longer and we both let go in unison. Luckily, my trickles were drowned out by the elephant's torrents, and it plodded off into the darkness, unaware of my presence.

"Gosh, darling, you were desperate. I could hear you from the tent!" Pattie commented.

"Mum, that was an elephant!"

She thought that I should've been more neighbourly and tossed a few squares of loo roll over the thatch for it to use. We giggled ourselves to sleep and it felt like minutes later that the breakfast gong rang at five o' clock sharp the next morning.

After a quick recce of Norman's car, I joined Emily at the campfire. She had made strong tea and thick porridge which always tasted better in the bush. I didn't reveal the silly events of the night to Clem, who was in a mood having left his rifle outside the tent after he turned off the lights last night and it was gone. He could tell by the spore that elephants had been through the camp and despatched his best tracker to follow the hyena paw prints into the bush to find his rifle.

Pattie emerged from the tent in a pair of khaki shorts, zebra print shirt and an enormous bush hat tied down under her chin with a bow. She held a clipboard in one hand and one of her crutches in the other. Clem was used to such visions from townies and from his expression, thought the outfit was over the top, especially wearing a zebra print in lion country but he continued to slurp his tea and didn't comment. His mood lifted when the tracker returned with his rifle, minus the leather case which the hyenas had probably had for dinner.

After checking the gun over for any damage, he tuned in the two-way radio to make comms with his son who was flying reconnaissance in search of rhinos. Emily explained that most visitors spent weeks waiting in camp for a sighting: two hundred thousand hectares of wilderness was a huge area to cover. Just as she began to describe the process of rhino capture, the speakers crackled.

"Mother and calf, 15 clicks north-east of camp. Over!"

Clem tossed his tea to the floor and sprang into action. On the run, he told us to gather the camera equipment, fast! Pattie was instructed to climb in the front seat of the Land Rover, next to his tracker and Ian and I jumped in the back with the rest of his team. Through the sliding window I could hear Clem telling Pattie that we would follow the dirt road as far as possible, then go off road and on foot if required. That was all the information she was given; he was too distracted listening to the radio.

The morning air was icy, and the open back of the

Land Rover shook violently as we sped along bumpy roads, following coordinates. I was almost lost to the wilds when we swerved off into thick bush at full speed without warning. Pattie glanced back at me with her hat flapping against her face, she was in pain. Her new hip replacement was taking a hammering. The radio crackled again, and Clem dropped a gear, charging over saplings, anthills, and anything else that was in his way screeching to a stop at the top of a hill.

The team sprang out the back and belly crawled to the edge of the hilltop without saying a word. Ian and I copied them, but all Pattie could do was remain by the passenger door, unable to move her leg. Clem searched the area through his binoculars and signalled the number one and a half to his men. He loaded his rifle with a tranquilizer dart and shot the adult rhino who fled with her baby in the opposite direction to us.

The team erupted from their crouching position and sprinted downhill through the bush after it. I made chase but my heavy breathing soon steamed-up the viewfinder on the camera and I struggled to follow blurs of bodies and smudges of trees and shrubs. When the chase changed direction for a third time my language deteriorated slightly. I could hear the thunderous steps of a frightened animal but had no idea if I was about to be flattened by a rhino, her calf or Clem's lightning swift team. When the drug eventually took effect, the creature fell asleep with her head resting in the tree fork of a mopane, four kilometres away from our starting point!

Clem rushed over and covered her eyes with his hat and checked the animal over. He took blood samples, horn measurements and strapped a tracking collar around her neck before an enormous 35 tonne truck appeared from nowhere and winched the animal on board with a harness. The rest of the team encircled the calf who'd been hovering nearby. They attached a lasso and cajoled it up a ramp to join its mother. I stood there, stunned at what I'd just witnessed: the skill, dedication and tenderness shown by them all was incredible.

With both animals safely on board, Clem turned on his heels and ran back through the bush to collect the Land Rover. Ian and I caught a lift with the rhinos and managed to get several close-up shots on a difficult bumpy road home. Clem and Pattie were already at the boma[19] when the truck reversed into position and the rhino was winched off into the shade. By the time she started to rouse, her baby was by her side.

The mood was jovial around the campfire that evening. Clem gushed on about the planned relocation of mother and calf while Emily warmed up left-over impala stew for dinner. Pattie reviewed the footage and I apologised for any bad language she might have heard. She put the tapes sequentially into a box and wrote the words *SOS Black Rhino* on her clipboard. A simple statement that became the title of this documentary.

We were incredibly lucky to witness the capture of another three rhinos during our 10 days in Ruckomechi and running the gauntlet through the bush became old hat! Clem rescued an incredible young bull that constantly tried to break out by charging the wooden boma fence. The rebound sent me tumbling from my filming advantage point a few times. Extra timber was used to reinforce the perimeter to make sure that this beauty didn't escape. The two other rescues were young calves, both were found hovering around their butchered mothers. It was disgusting and heart-breaking to see. I couldn't fathom what possible ridiculous medicinal purpose their mothers' horns could have for humans to justify that brutality.

---

19. An enclosure used to secure livestock and wildlife.

One calf stood motionless near its mother, ignored by the poachers because it hadn't grown a horn yet. Its ears had been ripped off in a fight with a pack of hyenas that were eating its mother's carcass. We named him Big Ears. The other baby we named Noddy. She bobbed her head, nudging her mother's dead body for milk, which was still warm when we arrived.

I spent hours filming their antics in the nursery, and Pattie used some of the footage in a teaser campaign to pre-launch *SOS Black Rhino*. The advert showed Big Ears and Noddy playing in their pen chasing each other in circles to the song *"Ring a Ring o' Roses"*, a clip of Noddy bobbing her head was synced to the words *"atishoo atishoo"*, but instead of the words *"we all fall down"* Pattie cut in the sound of a shotgun with the footage of their butchered mothers and left viewers stunned.

Noddy and Big Ears became the breeding herd for Imire Rhino and Wildlife Conservancy in Wedza. When Pattie made a documentary about the conservancy a few years later, Noddy and Big Ears were fully grown and she revelled in the small part she'd played, calling them by name and fully expecting them to come bounding up to her!

SOS Black Rhino created a huge amount of awareness and put Pattie at the forefront of the Ride for Rhino campaign which followed shortly afterwards. She flew around the world arranging photographic shoots and PR functions for the Rhino Girls, Charlie Hewat and Julie Edwards, who were cycling from England to Zimbabwe to raise funds. The nation watched and prayed as they cycled past war zones and through deserts. Pattie met Elton John, David Essex and Zambian President, Kenneth Kaunda, during the campaign and appeared in the press with daily reports on the Girls' progress. The Rhino Girls received the heroes' welcome they deserved and watching Pattie standing on her crutches surrounded by dignitaries at the finish line, I hoped to become at least half the woman she was. I joined Julie at university the following year to study journalism in the hope of becoming as good as my mother.

****

22

When I arrived in Grahamstown in 1988, apartheid[20] was being denounced around the world; anti-apartheid limpet mines were going off in every South African city and student protests cried out for the release of Nelson Mandela. On 3 March around one thousand students and academics marched through campus protesting the government's banning of 17 anti-apartheid organisations. Julie and I clambered to the rooftops and watched events unfold from afar. Foreign student study visas would be revoked for participating and it made my degree in journalism feel fake.

To make matters worse, Zimbabwe's increasingly difficult foreign exchange controls were making it hard for Pattie and Norman to fund my studies. I received 50 Rand a month for pocket money (US$0.50) and was as poor as a church mouse. Zimbabwean freedom of speech laws also made me doubt whether I would even be able to practice the profession when I got back home. I yearned to be out in the field with my mother earning a living and doing anything other than clambering on rooftops. Feelings that were exacerbated when I watched the momentous Papal visit to Zimbabwe on a small television alone in my university digs. South Africa had been pointedly excluded from the itinerary as the Pope strongly condemned apartheid.

When Pope John Paul II kissed the tarmac at Harare airport, the country shook with excitement and Catholic

---

20. Institutional racial segregation.

societies throughout Africa pulsated with faith and joy. I couldn't help but think of my Gran, who'd missed his visit by just three years. She would've chased him through the streets waving her knitting needles in the air. Pattie, however, made up for her absence by presenting the pontiff with her film on the history of the Catholic Society in Zimbabwe. The photograph of her holding his hand at Harare Cathedral, was enlarged to its maximum and displayed prominently in the lounge entrance at Esher Close. It was impossible to decide who in the picture looked happier.

After visiting Botswana, the Pope's plane was heading to Lesotho when the weather turned nasty. The storm knocked out the navigation beacons and radio signals in Maseru and his plane had to be re-routed to Johannesburg to refuel. The world watched him descend the aircraft steps of the apartheid infested Jan Smuts Airport where he refrained from kissing the ground, despite having such a bad flight. I thought I'd have an opportunity to cover some of his bizarre unplanned visit to South Africa, but he was whisked away in an armoured vehicle and immediately left for Maseru by road. When he was canonized 26 years later, Pattie' became the first person in our family history to have touched the hand of a Catholic saint, and she had the photograph to prove it! No doubt my Gran watched the canonization ceremony from Heaven, with Pope John Paul II by her side, forcibly and resplendently dressed in her papal balaclava and mittens, at last!

I was still floundering on the university rooftops when Maureen was diagnosed with terminal cancer. She refused treatment and wanted her body left to science. Her other wish was to learn to drive before she died. Pattie took her to lessons twice a week where she was surprisingly devilish behind the wheel, but too poorly to sit the final exam. She spent her last days in my bedroom, surrounded by the art rosettes we had won due to her persistence over the years.

A Bible and draft version of her French dictionary were in the bedside drawer. The funeral parlour struggled to get her gurney through the tight, crooked passageways of Esher Close, which Norman decided couldn't be fixed unless the entire house was pulled down. "Mon Dieu, quel problème ai-je causé?" (Good Heavens, what trouble have I caused?) I imagined Maureen saying.

The following year Nelson Mandela was finally released after serving 27 years in prison. Student protests turned to celebrations as he walked the Grand Parade in Cape Town, and the dismantling of apartheid began.

In 1991, Pattie received both the Television and the Radio Presenter of the Year awards. At her acceptance speech for the first award, she said "my children are my finest production." I felt unworthy of the accolade, having abandoned Journalism altogether. Her speech was also tainted with sadness after the death of her middle sister, Angela. I was glad to be home offering support by then, but it felt a sadder place. Women I'd known all my life were gone.

I started coaching the women's hockey team at Alexandra Sports Club, which is where I met Vicki for the first time. She spent many evenings around the lazy Susan, becoming an integral part of our family and an important part of my life. Pattie and Norman loved her company and treated her like a surrogate daughter. Through her, I got a job in marketing at a tobacco warehousing company and with it came my first taste of financial freedom. Five years later, I joined the Dulux marketing department and a wonderful life in the paint industry began.

"Oh, darling, we spent all that money at university for you to watch paint dry,' Pattie giggled.

Through Vicki, I joined Sherwood Golf Club where she was Lady Captain and a talented golfer. I met many lifelong friends at Sherwood, including Pat, Janis and Charmaine.

As I slipped into adulthood, we travelled the country playing competitive golf, meeting wonderful people and making incredible memories. Pattie transferred her enthusiasm and support from my hockey to the golf course, and frequently appeared from behind trees near the putting green with her camera.

"Hello darlings," she called.

****

23

In 1992, Zimbabwe experienced its worst drought on record. Crops failed and millions of people needed food aid. More than one million head of cattle perished, and wildlife was either poached for food or died of starvation and thirst. Pattie couldn't bear to witness children begging for food or fainting on their walk to school, so she opened a soup kitchen at Hatcliffe Extension squatter camp and our kitchen became the production hub for a continuous cycle of stews and soups. Her recipes were unmeasured and difficult to repeat. Spices were identified by a good sniff and sprinkled into the pot using instinct rather than a teaspoon, but her food was delicious, and the hungry children wolfed it down. The oven warming drawer was crammed with trays of old tea bags being dried out for reuse at the soup kitchen and a variety of oddly shaped biscuits cooled on racks on every countertop. "A cup of tea fixes everything, you know!"

Pattie invariably sang while she was cooking and if Norman recognised the song, he would join in, bellowing from the lounge. Even *"Non, je ne regrette rien"* warbled occasionally. The words no longer held the same connotations, but the song remained one of Pattie's favourites and still received groans from Christianne and me!

As the demand for food in the soup kitchen grew, Pattie decided to keep chickens and rabbits on the steep slopes of Esher Close and started a *Butcher in your own backyard* scheme. As an avid animal lover Christianne felt this was a step too far, but our mother said it was vital.

"A child cannot learn on an empty stomach," she exclaimed.

Norman built her a sturdy abattoir well hidden from view behind the fir trees and Lovebug often giggled about her chickens and rabbits developing one leg shorter than the other to remain upright on her hill. Once the butchery was opened, if a suspicious looking stew arrived on our dinner table, Christianne and I would burst into song with the tune from *Watership Down*, *"Bright Eyes"*. Norman sang along each time to show solidarity, but really loved a bit of rabbit stew, especially when it was dressed in his perfectly built abattoir.

Our scullery became a storeroom for another of Pattie's projects called *There's no such thing as rubbish!* It overflowed with plastic containers, cardboard boxes and toilet roll holders that she'd received from church appeals. The plastic containers were filled with borehole water and distributed to the squatter camp which had no access to clean water and with the drought, had little or no river water to use either. The paper products were kept for the children's art and craft classes and church members were constantly astonished when Pattie received their rubbish with absolute delight.

"Waste not want not!" She responded.

On Christmas day, every piece of wrapping paper was saved, and the hundreds of cards she received were cut up for the schoolchildren to make collages. Present boxes were flattened and saved including her very special Chanel No 5-perfume box. Norman dressed up as Father Christmas each year and after handing out traditional glasses of sherry he presented Lovebug with her favourite perfume, every year without fail. Pattie accentuated her surprise each time it was unwrapped.

"It's delicious, Mister!" she said, giving us all a quick squirt to affirm its loveliness.

On one of her Hatcliffe runs, she spotted the artistic potential in a young man called David, one of seven children born to an agricultural labourer. She got him to submit a portfolio to the BAT art workshop, which offered disadvantaged children an opportunity to formally develop their skills. She sponsored him, became his mentor, and he achieved an A for GCSE Art. Many of his paintings hung on our lounge walls in gratitude. David Chinyama became an international artist with a gallery in Canada and was Pattie's finest example of her social endeavours.

The President's wife, Sally Mugabe passed away that year. Pattie had met her through the Catholic Women's League shortly after independence. They were like-minded women with social welfare agendas. With the help from Sally's Child Survival and Development Foundation, they established the Kushinga Ladies Sewing Co-operative, providing skills and employment for residents in Hatcliffe. Together, they sourced funding for a film on the Mutemwa Leprosy Mission in Mutoko, with the aim of removing the stigma attached to the disease. They also started a Justice for Women campaign which fought for women's equality in the home and workplace, and they loved every minute of the fight.

In 1993, Pattie became the first woman to be awarded a Fellowship from the Zimbabwe Institute of Public Relations for her "contribution to good communication in all fields and for creating mutual understanding, knowledge, and goodwill.". Accepting the award, she said:

"Out of all the lovely things that have happened, this is one of the best. But I should have done more for the most important natural resource of any country – its people. I have come to realise that there is no point in asking people at survival level to save the last tree in the area when they have hungry children to feed. I would cut it down myself, build a fire and pray for a miracle tomorrow. It is useless to ask communities to attend meetings on early planting when they have no money for seed. During the

drought years in Zimbabwe, it filled me with rage to find little children collapsed on the road because they had not eaten in two days. Yet they were desperate not to miss a day at school.

So, I am devoting my golden years in Public Relations to people, to uplift their lives — to achieve their educational goals — to help create employment opportunities by raising funds to send youths for training. With the help of some donated old typewriters and paper we have set up a Hatcliffe secretarial service. We have mended and sold old sacks and collected empty bottles. There's no such thing as rubbish! Plastic containers, toilet roll holders, cardboard, and pieces of material for Grades 1 and 2 at Hatcliffe School. We have already had some success with twelve young men completing six weeks at the Institute of Agricultural Engineering and another gaining a place at the BAT (British American Tobacco) Art School."

With help from British Airways, Rotary, Borrowdale residents, the Zimbabwe Parents of Handicapped Children Association, and members of St Gerard's Church, she opened a day-care centre for disabled children in Hatcliffe, called 'Tambainesu' (Play with us). A twenty-foot container arrived, filled with medicines for the new polyclinic beside it, which was a godsend for the local community. A new appeal went out on the church notice board for used medicine bottles.

Norman's pumpkin growing endeavours finally made the news that year as well. Not because one had escaped from its vine and injured anyone, but a carefully nurtured 92-kilogramme monster had won him second prize in the Harare Men's Club pumpkin growing competition.

"Absolutely splendid!" he roared, at the prize-giving.

The picture of him wearing a tuxedo standing next to the beast was frequently spun around the lazy Susan for all to see. When the mutant veggie arrived home after the awards, Pattie rubbed her hands together with glee, a million plans for its distribution. Norman cut it into more manageable pieces with an electric saw and scooped out the phenomenal seeds for prosperity. The kitchen turned orange overnight with pumpkin soup, pumpkin fritters, pumpkin pie, pumpkin in every form for months afterwards.

Pattie's last project for Hatcliffe was an *Adopt a library* campaign. Requests for second-hand school and exercise books, were added to the church notices. By then, our house was running out of space, as was the church appeals board, and boxes spilled into Norman's pristine workshop. He was indifferent about most of the books but would often be found sitting on his workbench, mentally completing questions from the maths books and fixing the incorrect answers on the exercise sheets.

****

24

Towards the end of the 1990s Pattie produced and presented *The Heritage of Zimbabwe* series for television on a tight budget. The Conservation Trust relied on commercial contributions to make their films and their coffers were running low. Public Relations and promotional films had become a non-vital expense for businesses struggling to stay afloat in a deteriorating economy. Pattie wrote to every contact she had and through dogged determination, raised funds to produce her last series, *It's Your World, Zimbabwe*, showcasing its many beauty spots in the hope of boosting tourism.

She was made Rothmans Communicator of the Year for her "contribution to creating awareness of the need to conserve our environment and wildlife." The Paul Harris Award from Rotary International, for her efforts towards the "betterment of understanding and friendly relations among peoples of the world", encapsulated her. Norman proudly escorted her to the podium to receive the gold medal, deserving one himself for all the love and support and the completion of Esher Close house repairs, apart from the crooked passageway walls.

Pattie bolstered her income by writing double-page-spread feature articles for various national newspapers, but freelance writers were notoriously badly paid. From the bay window of Esher Close, she started to write her book, *The Last of the White Ants*. A fictional story about the daily lives of British colonial civil servants in Zomba. As the bills mounted, she watched friends and colleagues emigrate from

Zimbabwe, and considered for the first time that she might have to do the same.

Christianne fell in love and moved into the perfectly rebuilt cottage at the end of the garden. For a short time, Mr Bacon was part of our family which made introductions with the Pinks and Beans hysterical, but he wasn't around for long.

It was a fruitful decade with 10 grandchildren born. Norman would wrap his enormous wicketkeeper's hands around them for hugs, prompting several "be gentle" reprimands from Pattie. They hoped to have at least enough grandchildren for a cricket team and all eyes were on me. Despite having some amazing boyfriends, I was not ready to settle down and make their team complete.

By the end of the century, our government's military support for the Kabila regime in the Congo and a mismanaged domestic economic reform program, cost Zimbabweans billions. Mugabe faced growing opposition and lost a referendum on constitutional reforms. In response he organised an unbudgeted pay out for war veterans and used them to start invading white-owned commercial farms. The economy went down a slippery slide and Norman's meticulously planned pension was suddenly worth a loaf of bread.

He also needed an emergency triple bypass and a hip replacement, which was a very worrying time, but he spent many evenings explaining the fantastic mechanics of it all and came through it with no problems. Pattie had another two hip replacements: the third on one side and a first on the other leg. They now had five new hips between them, and it became a family joke for them to stop swinging from any chandeliers before more bones were damaged.

With the Zimbabwean dollar rapidly devaluing, the medical aid shortfall for all their operations used up most of their savings. Despite pouring several large cups of tea, they could no longer manage. After much soul searching, they decided to move back to England after a combined 100 years in Africa. Ironically Pattie had just been made an Honorary Life Member of the Zimbabwe Institute of Public Relations.

It was a mammoth task, clearing the contents of their home. Selecting which belongings to keep was agonizing. The Malawian carvings, a couple of David's paintings and the picture of Pope John Paul II, were the first to be packed. We held open days to sell everything else and Pattie's heart broke watching her dream home being stripped, bit by bit. I often found her crying in her bedroom, looking out at the hibiscus bush where Ringo Star lay.

Her friend, Wyn Hooper, painted a picture of the view from Esher Close and Pattie planned to hang it up in England where she could look at it every day. Norman sold his Mercedes and an immaculate collection of tools from his workshop. The only thing left behind was the old family tin trunk which was filled with Pattie's writing that she hoped I'd read someday. The contents were to become the source of much of the information that I used to tell her story.

They were both pushed through the airport in wheelchairs. Pattie turned and waved as they passed through customs.

"Come visit soon, darling," she called.

Zimbabwe had lost a national treasure. They left in 2001 with two suitcases each and travelled via South Africa to say goodbye to Bin and Pieter on their farm in Warmbaths. Bin had been diagnosed with Parkinson's disease and shook like a leaf. The next time they would meet, Pattie's gentle loving sister would be in a home, comatose.

"Don't ever put me in one of those," Pattie made me promise.

Christianne married her second husband, Graham, and they too left for England with Joshua and their new baby,

Scott. Norman and Pattie finally had enough grandchildren for their own cricket team which was personally a relief but suddenly Margaret, Christopher and my cousins, Elizabeth and James, were the last of my family left in Zimbabwe with me.

****

25

Pattie and Norman settled near Christianne in Ipswich, Suffolk but they were hardly at home for the first year, visiting family and friends across England and Europe. There was added joy when their twelfth grandchild, Benjamin, was born. The hospital gynaecologist on call that day had also immigrated from Zimbabwe and bizarrely enough, was the same specialist at Christianne's side for the birth of her two previous children in Harare. They greeted each other like old friends in the elevator going up to surgery and he asked her to sing the first verse of the Zimbabwe National Anthem as he inserted the epidural needle into her spine. A small world indeed.

Norman loved his new life. He had thick newspapers to read every day, a bounty of live cricket games on television and no repairs or crooked passageways to attend to in their rented accommodation. After a thorough examination of the engine, he bought a second-hand Vauxhall Astra and could be found outside in all kinds of weather, tinkering with it. They felt secure for the first time in a while, and from afar realised how quickly their quality of life had been eroded in Zimbabwe. Deep baths were poured, lights were turned on freely and what money they had in the bank didn't evaporate. Pattie was again grateful to Queen Elizabeth II for her assistance with housing and benefits and recalled the story of the breast milk run in Malawi whenever Her Majesty appeared on television.

Once the welcome visits were over, Pattie found the daily

routine of retirement dull. To keep busy she plotted places to visit from a road map of Britain and they'd set off on regular adventures armed with several packets of Jelly Babies in case they got lost. Norman would drive wherever she wanted to go and postcards of visits to the Needles, Harry's Rock, castles, and museums arrived in our post.

After almost a decade travelling around Africa in small aeroplanes, I'd developed a fear of flying. To remain on terra firma, I left Dulux and opened a paint retail and decorating business in Harare. Vicki and my friend, Lisa, became shareholders and we had plans to make a fortune and retire at 50. For the first few years we were on track, but in 2007 a new monetary policy caused chapters on hyperinflation to be re-written into economic theory.

By 2008 we were dealing in billions and trillions of Zimbabwe dollars. Calculators no longer held enough digits and accounting packages had to be redesigned to accommodate all the zeros. In total, 26 zeros were gained and lost from our currency and the magnitude of the inflation led to the country's unprecedented economic meltdown. Each time our currency changed, business accounts had to be balanced off and a new set of accounts opened. If my school maths teacher had pitched a blackboard duster at me then, I would've pinned it straight back at her.

Income devalued by the hour, pensions and savings evaporated. Businesses couldn't afford to increase salaries at the same rate as inflation and living expenses became unsustainable. It was illegal to deal in foreign currency but almost impossible to keep up with the devaluation of the Zimbabwe dollar. It became more profitable to hoard and necessities disappeared from supermarket shelves. On one occasion I popped into a renowned supermarket chain in search of milk and every shelf was stacked with nothing other than light bulbs! A product made redundant by power cuts that ran for three-quarters of the day.

Seedy warehouses opened in back alleys selling household basics in hard currency at a higher rate than the official Reserve Bank figure. Barter trade flourished: I traded paint for flour to make bread for staff teas, sold paint to farmers who paid with sacks of dressed chickens which were swapped for fuel. Most transactions were in bulk, and the excess of one product could be bartered for another.

One product that everyone needed was the humble toilet roll which vendors sold from pedestrian islands at every set of traffic lights. The toilet roll exchange became a thriving business where currency was handed out of car windows and bulk packets of toilet rolls were tossed back in return. It was oddly comforting knowing that loo rolls were so accessible.

When the Reserve Bank stopped minting coins and smaller note denominations, cheap commodities such as eggs, matches, sweets and pens were used to give customers change. Each item carried a value and customers could choose what *change* they needed most. Motor vehicle consoles soon overflowed with change in various forms and accounting documents became interesting reading. Petty cash slips for 10 chickens = 20 litres of fuel or change = four eggs! The back rooms of the paint shop started to fill up with everything other than paint. Bucket-loads of humour spilled over the counter where egg baskets and sweet jars had replaced the till.

I returned to the shop one day after a site visit and Vicki popped out from behind the counter and handed me a Maltese-cross-terrier puppy. I thought for a minute that it was the result of some bartering deal, but she had rescued the terrified creature from an abusive home. He was blind in one eye and only had partial sight in the other. I hadn't owned an animal for years but when his smile revealed three teeth, my heart melted. I named him Scruffy, and he became my chief bodyguard just like Ringo Star had been for Pattie. Shortly afterwards, I got a Jack Russell called Muffin, as company for him. The dogs were never far from me and became part of our business brand – just miniature, noisier versions of the Dulux English sheepdog.

Muffin invariably had a toy in her mouth and dropped it for anyone willing to play. It was not unusual for her to plonk it out of the window at the toilet roll exchange for the vendors to toss back along with the toilet rolls. Scruffy simply found the whole transaction an ordeal and charged the window every time.

I met my partner, Jules, during this time, and we made a beautiful home together in Borrowdale just as the Government failed to pay its debts and the infrastructure of the country collapsed. Lines of credit for imported electricity were paused and power outages ran for 18 hours a day. What little electricity we did receive was squeezed out of the exhausted turbines of Lake Kariba hydroelectric power station. The water level of the dam shrank to its lowest in history as a result.

The sale of solar panels, inverter battery systems and generators soared. Most businesses and homes operated on a combination of all of them. For a time, gas was also an option, if you could afford to pay Z$220 billion a kilogram on the black market. Replacing the stock was almost impossible and the country soon ran out. Those who couldn't afford alternative power sources relied on a dodgy load-shedding schedule. Electricity usually came on for brief periods at ungodly hours when a nation of midnight crawlers emerged from their beds to bake birthday cakes, iron clothes or to mow the lawn in their pyjamas.

Water supply was a big concern, we could do without almost anything but not that. Local reservoirs rarely received enough electricity for the pumps to build up pressure, and when it did, the badly maintained pipes lost a lot of the water. I had an 80-metre-deep borehole sunk in the garden and the water plumbed into a 5000-litre tank with a pump that was linked to every alternative power system in the house. If the borehole dried up during the dry season, a variety of bulk water delivery services obliged and became a booming industry. When all this failed, we had a swimming pool to bath in, and weather pleasant enough to light a wood fire outside and boil that vital cup of tea to "fix everything."

Local councils reduced services by 75% and what little they could provide came at incredible cost. Property taxes, municipal water, garbage collection, sewage disposal and electricity increased from Z$2,902,676,000 a month to Z$42,275,000,000 fifteen days later. Almost a 1500 percent increase!

Municipalities had no funds for repairs and maintenance. When streetlights were knocked over through car accidents or fell because of rust, they were pushed off the road and left to rot. Potholes in the roads became trenches which were filled by volunteers using discarded bricks. They held up cardboard signs saying *"Pliz Help"* and begged for donations. Drivers tossed out whatever *change* lay in their consoles, grateful to them for a passable, albeit cobbled, road.

In January 2008, our shop sold 20 litres of Dulux wall paint for Z$617,628,231 and by June the same year, the same product sold for Z$1,471,959,674,598 - that's one trillion, four hundred and seventy-one billion, nine hundred and fifty-nine million, six hundred and seventy-four thousand, five hundred and ninety-eight dollars. Fortunately, nobody accepted cheques, so figures like that never had to be written out!

As the farm invasions intensified, more farmers were murdered or chased off their land by supposed war veterans that seemed too young to have participated in the Liberation

War. Farm production collapsed, and Zimbabwe headed for a humanitarian crisis as the nation began to starve. Anyone on a fixed income or without access to hard currency found it almost impossible to support themselves.

Janis and Charmaine had taken over the running of the bar at Avondale Club and we met up with them there every Tuesday. The membership was mostly pensioners, and we witnessed their struggles first-hand. Economic social isolation was prevalent amongst the elderly but one woman we knew was determined to visit the club once a week. She bought a tot of cheap gin for Z$2.8 billion (US$3) but couldn't afford the mixer. Most of her pension went on food for her dog. A gin at the club once a week was her only treat and her only interaction. Janis made sure she got a mixer for free.

Tony was a close friend of Vicki's and a veteran of the battle of El Alamein in World War II. He was too proud to ask her for help and walked to the British Embassy in Harare, handed over his passport and declared himself destitute. The British Government took cognisance of the plight of an estimated 3000 vulnerable elderly nationals over the age of 70 and offered them free repatriation to the UK. Within a few weeks, Tony was on a one-way flight to a veterans' lodge in Horsham. Our office manager and Sherwood golfing friend, Pat, also accepted the offer and was sent to sheltered accommodation in Swindon.

Pensioners without an option to be re-settled in Britain survived on the breadline and relied on charities like SOAP (Save Old Age Pensioners) to provide meals. Jules and I organised social evenings at home which allowed pensioners to get out and have a hot meal with a projected movie or an amateur variety performance. Most of our friends were cajoled into doing a skit of some sort to fill up the evening. At one show, Vicki and her friend, Sarah, both played guitars and sang an hilarious version of *"Kumbaya,"* and repeatedly appeared on stage with another verse to fill in the gaps. Noreen was too shy to be on stage but played *"Three Blind Mice"* on the recorder from behind the lounge curtain. Rosemary did a lively line dance with a group of friends. Jules and I dressed up as geisha girls and played the *"The Flower Duet"* on the piano, singing the words in Japanese. Most of the skits were so ridiculous that audiences were left in stitches demanding an encore!

Animals also suffered during this time which was a cause close to Janis' heart. Avondale Club became a food donation hub for organisations like the Friend Foundation, the ZNSPCA, SPCA and the Veterinarians for Animal Welfare Society (VAWS). Scruffy and Muffin's five-in-one vaccinations that year cost Z$42 billion and, because dog food was unavailable in the shops, we fed them Kudu mince, bought in bulk from a farmer down the road.

Jules and I started a side-line to help our elderly friends obtain household basics. We were soon sourcing baking ingredients, and they earned a little money selling home-made milk tarts, chocolate cakes and jams from the paint shop counter. We called the side-line, Maka-Plan (make-a-plan), a tag-on that described every Zimbabwean living in a volatile economy. The paint shop became a hotspot for people to meet, make plans and recount stories of the latest incredible saga in obtaining necessities. If a product was unavailable, secret family recipes were exchanged on how to make things like floor polish, candles, window cleaner, self-raising-flour or how to bake bread in a cast iron pot over a fire.

Alcohol was mostly available on the black market in 5-litre plastic containers. The chigubhu[21] lived in the boot of your car and was brought out like an accessory at gatherings. Your name had to be printed onto it because they all looked

---

21. Shona word for bottle.

identical, and the levels were constantly eyeballed because of the difficulty in replacing it. Friends and family overseas thought we were bonkers, but Zimbabweans are remarkably adaptable and resilient. Few complained, everybody helped each other and, together with a great sense of humour, we got by.

****

26

Zimbabweans withdrew every cent possible from their bank accounts and converted it to hard currency or anything that held its value longer than the Zimbabwe dollar. Queues for cash snaked around all the banks, especially on pay days. Businesses started paying bills using bank transfers which had about a 40 percent surcharge because of the amount it devalued between crediting and debiting an account. Companies could only draw a maximum of Z$25 billion in cash a day, which equated to 25 loaves of bread. Individuals could only withdraw Z$10 billion a day. Two-tier charging systems developed, offering a discount for cash and a premium for bank transfers. Church offertory baskets remained empty unless God accepted a bank transfer or a variety of *change!*

If not for Mrs Kamba I would've queued at the bank for 16 full days to pay for a fuel filter that I'd sourced at a cash price of Z$161 billion dollars. I almost hugged her when she arrived at the shop, pulling a suitcase on wheels containing Z$125 quintillion in cash to pay for her house to be painted inside and out. It took five hours to count, and the counting machine nearly blew a bearing. Mrs Kamba sold me her suitcase for one million Zimbabwe dollars just so I could carry it all.

When the contract started, the cost of a commuter taxi for the painters to get to work was Z$7 billion one way per passenger. 5 kilograms of maize meal cost Z$50 billion, 1 kilogramme of sugar and 1 litre of oil cost Z$40 billion each. If we paid the regulated wage of Z$148 million a month, the painters would starve. We started to pay them in food packs and more space was filled with commodities at the paint shop. Mrs Kamba's contract was completed in 10 days, by which time the same taxi ride for the painters to get to work, cost Z$50 billion and we sent them all on annual leave until something changed.

To save the Government printing press from blowing up in smoke, a 20-billion dollar Special Agro-cheque was introduced. This temporarily reduced the wads of cash we had to carry around in Mrs Kamba's suitcase but meant that our sweet jars bulged with more change. A 100 trillion-dollar note had to be introduced and became the largest denomination of currency ever issued. A 25-billion dollar Agro-cheque followed somewhere amongst all of this and there was every possibility that we could move to quadrillions and sextillions. Haggling for prices in quads or sexes would have been interesting! Year -on-year inflation reached a milestone at 89 sextillion percent (21 zeros!).

The dire state of the country was continually blamed on the sanctions imposed by America and Britain, who wanted our government to respect democratic principles and to comply with international human rights law. The March Presidential elections were Mugabe's toughest electoral challenge yet and a crippled nation leant towards the reform promises of Morgan Tsvangirai, the leader of the Movement for Democratic Change Party (MDC). When American and British diplomats travelled to the rural areas to check that voting was free and fair, they were harassed at police roadblocks and detained for several hours. The incident was raised with the UN Security Council and humanitarian aid to the country was suspended.

As tension rose, foreign nationals living in Zimbabwe were advised to register family members with their embassies in preparation for an evacuation. My relationship with Jules was considered illegal outside the Embassy gates but I scurried to the car wearing dark glasses after registering her as my life partner and phoned her immediately with the news.

"I've told the Queen about us! What's that they say about go big or go home!"

Foreign nationals kept a suitcase packed for the month that it took to release the official election results. Morgan Tsvangirai was declared the winner, but without a sufficient majority, a run-off election was required. Mugabe's power had been impregnable for 28 years and he was irritated. The period prior to the run-off was tainted with political violence, intimidation and disappearances. Farm invasions were rampant, squatter camps were pulled down to push the people back into their tribal lands, where Mugabe had more control through the chiefs. Hatcliffe squatter camp was included and Pattie was inconsolable when she heard the news.

"Why, darling, why?" she cried.

It was during this time that I travelled with Vicki to attend her uncle's funeral at his farm in Chinhoyi. A month prior, the farm had been invaded by war veterans, but he'd refused to leave and the stress of it was thought to have contributed to his death.

The graveside funeral near the farmhouse overlooked Mike's favourite view but each time his grave was dug, the war veterans filled it in. Under the shade of a few acacia trees, the priest shouted out his sermon above their chants and asked the congregation to sing loudly. A spirited chorus of *"How Great Thou Art"* belted out across the land. The whole affair was rowdy: the louder the war veterans chanted, the louder we sang. On the third attempt to bury him, we got as far as a procession to the grave. A piper gallantly strutted ahead playing *"Oh Flower of Scotland"*, but we were forced to retreat again. The coffin was placed temporarily under a tree, and the priest directed us into the farmhouse for tea, as you do. In the meantime, Mike's wife, Alice, negotiated a price of two cattle, four goats, and a few billion dollars and her husband's body was finally committed to the disputed earth. The farm was expropriated shortly afterwards.

A few days later, Pattie's elderly friend, Nicky phoned to say that her house had burnt down! She had gone out with her book club for the day and had accidentally left on a plate on the stove during a power outage. In her absence power came back on and a dish towel caught alight. Fire engines arrived without any water in their tankers and by the time they suctioned it from a neighbour's swimming pool, it was too late. Two generations of British Army memorabilia had burnt to the ground. Nicky was stoical about the whole ordeal and said that she needed to downsize anyway. 20 years of filing as secretary for the Borrowdale Ratepayers' Association had also gone up in smoke, which she thought delightful!

While all this was going on, Pattie and Norman had moved from Ipswich into a third-floor flat in sheltered accommodation in Dorset. Pattie phoned to let me know that she had fallen, broken her leg at the top of her femur and dislodged the third hip replacement. A fourth hip replacement on that side would require pioneering surgery as well as a donor femur of the same length and density as her current leg. Pattie didn't care what was needed, she was so excited that she would still be able to walk upright.

"Fabulous news, darling. We've found a right femur at a bone bank in Leicester!"

It took a while for me to digest what she had just said. We couldn't buy milk from a corner store and my mother had just found herself a suitable leg!

"That's incredible Mum," I said, snuffling a laugh.

The Registrar of Addenbrookes Hospital listened to Pattie's

descriptions of her previous hip operations in Zimbabwe and mentioned that he had in fact married a Zimbabwean. After tossing around a few names and familiar places Pattie realised that he had married Bella, my tenacious, cat-suited friend from Chisipite Senior School. Bella had followed her dream to become a paediatric nurse and when she got the news from her husband, she insisted that Norman come to stay with her during and after Pattie's 10-hour pioneering surgery. They spent the evenings together having glasses of wine and reminiscing about the fantastic times they had spent together around the lazy Susan at Esher Close. Having Bella and Nish on the front-line during Pattie's operation was a godsend.

Back home, a constitutional amendment made it legal for the two main political parties to sign a painful power-sharing deal. A new democratic constitution was released which included gay rights for the first time, but it turned out to be political rhetoric and was left unratified. Overnight quintillions of Zimbabwe dollars disappeared from the balance sheets and the United States dollar became legal tender. For a time, sanity returned to the economy: shelves filled up again, toilet rolls vanished from traffic lights, fuel flowed from garage pumps for the first time in five years, flights became more affordable, and I could fly to England for a fleeting visit to check up on Pattie after her fantastic operation. Vicki decided to join me to check up on our repatriated friends, Tony and Pat. She also provided a strong arm for me to squeeze during the ten-hour flight.

****

Green Stamps for Heaven

27

Pattie looked pale and thin but was delighted to be upright after the operation, albeit a bit wobbly. She'd worn herself out going up and down the passageway to the lift to be the first in the foyer to greet us.

The interior of their flat was a miniature replica of Esher Close in Zimbabwe; warm, cosy, and familiar. One of David's paintings hung above the fireplace and a framed collage of Pattie's portfolio from Silhouette Modelling Studios hung in the dining room. Block-mounted pictures of the masked Gule Wamkulu dancers from Malawi hung in the passageway. One of the pictures had been used for the front cover of her book, which had been published. A copy had been placed on each bed in the spare room, next to a welcoming packet Jelly Babies. The photograph of Pope John Paul II took centre stage at the entrance and the painting of her beloved Esher Close hung above her desk. She said you could smell the grass and wheatfields on cold, dreary English days. Photographs of her 12 grandchildren smiled down at her from a bookshelf. Everything appeared normal, except Pattie had stopped driving since acquiring someone else's right femur.

"Darling, what if it came from a racing car driver?" she chuckled.

Norman was in fine kettle, sitting at a small table in the kitchen, eating a late breakfast of muesli with chopped apple and yoghurt. He moved to his favourite chair afterwards and started reading the papers front-to-back. While Vicki and I unpacked, Pattie browsed through emails on her new computer, which she used fervently to keep in touch with family and friends around the world. Their wall calendar was crammed with reminders of birthdays and special occasions. A thick A4 file, labelled *Pattie's Address Book*, stood out on the desk, and contained handwritten updated contact details of anyone she had ever met.

"How is your email working, Mum?" I asked.

A few weeks earlier, she had sent me an email which bounced back, and she replied to the Google postmaster notification by asking for help to contact her daughter in Zimbabwe. To our surprise, the "lovely" postmaster responded by suggesting that she try again but changed the extension of my email address from UK to ZW. In the meantime, I was pinged by the postmaster, who told me to get hold of my mother!

Pattie had the internet for the first time and its handy search engines opened a new world of adventure and exploration. Google Maps presented her with directions at the press of a button and made her chief navigator in the car, but they often got lost. After 25 years of marriage Norman understood that this was part of the adventure. I suggested that they bought a satnav which he thought was a marvellous idea, but Pattie said it would spoil all the fun.

I spent the first morning catching up with my brother Mark, while Pattie and Norman took Vicki on her first adventure to find the New Forest ponies. Pattie remembered that Vicki had been awarded Rhodesian colours for Gymkhana as a teenager and thought the ponies would be of interest to her. They ended up on the road to Bournemouth and, after two frustrating hours, had not seen anything with four legs. Vicki eventually made Norman pull over and took over driving herself. Rather than listening to Pattie's verbal instructions, she followed the signposts back to Ringwood and straight to a pub for them all to calm down!

The following day, Norman and Pattie needed to be in Somerset to attend her cousin's 90th birthday party. Vicki willingly jumped in the driver's seat to prevent a recurrence of yesterday debacle, but Pattie had already downloaded a map and remained chief navigator in the passenger seat. She had chosen the garden route so we could see something of the countryside and avoid the monotony of the highway. The journey was beautiful, and her directions were perfect.

On the way there I learnt that they had joined the British Legion Social Club for entertainment once a month. Norman had made friends with several retired army engineers, who dissected the workings of fantastic engines over a few glasses of wine. Pattie found that dull but said they had seen some amazing sites around the country. The Pump House in Bath after a boat trip down the Avon River; Norman's old classroom at Dulwich College where several renditions of his school song were sung in the car afterwards. The HMS Victory at Portsmouth Historic Harbour was fascinating, but Pattie struggled with her crutches in the small spaces. They had been over to France on the ferry but driving on the left-hand side of the road and asking for directions in French added many miles and unscheduled fuel stops to the trip. "C'est la vie, Mister," became Pattie's favourite response to the mounting fuel bill.

After a quick introduction to Cousin Bernard, Vicki and I left them at the front door and explored an antiques farm show for the afternoon. They both looked exhausted after the lengthy meal and Vicki agreed to drive back so long as Pattie chose the fastest route home. Her directions were so confusing that Vicki eventually pulled the car over and refused to go a step further until she looked at the map herself.

We visited Tony in Horsham, and Pat in Swindon. Both

were settled and well and had been astonished by the support and generosity that the British government had given them. After another failed attempt at seeing the New Forest ponies Vicki and I returned to Zimbabwe having spent five exhausting days in England, but we were satisfied that our loved ones were content and happy in their new homes. I put Pattie's diabolical map-reading down to age and pain, but it was not long after our return that I started to struggle to get hold of them.

They were never home, and my mother's adventure-seeking was out of control. Purchasing their first mobile phone helped for a while, but both wore hearing aids which made conversations difficult.

"Are you both alright?" I shouted down the phone to Norman.

"Mum can't sit still, darling. Her leg hurts but she doesn't complain, and the morphine helps." He said, sounding tired.

The news that my mother was taking oral morphine was a shock and could explain why they got so lost on their travels, but then Pattie sent an urgent email out to our family around the world, suggesting an impromptu reunion in France. With one month's notice the plan flopped and, disillusioned, she asked Norman to immediately drive her to Ipswich instead. Christianne got home from work, to find them on her doorstep.

Two weeks later, she invited Christianne and Mark for a night at Mont St Michel in France. The ferry left at seven in the morning; Pattie set her alarm for one o' clock. Norman insisted it was too early, but she would hear none of it, anxious not to be late. They sat in the dark, vacant car park, hungry and cold, for five hours before the ferry departed.

While all this was going on, Jules' mother Colleen and her friend Noreen had arrived in Zimbabwe, and we were taking them on a houseboat holiday on Lake Kariba. Christianne,

Benjamin, and Scott were flying out in a week's time to join us and when Pattie heard about it, she invited herself and announced that she and Norman would be arriving in Harare in three days' time. I thought she simply didn't want to miss out. Jules and I were thrilled our parents would finally meet, albeit unplanned and with a bit of juggling, the houseboat trip was re-organised to accommodate them.

They were both pushed out of Harare airport in wheelchairs. Pattie was dressed in a matching zebra print skirt and shirt with a wide-brimmed bush hat on her head. She pulled two 20-pound notes from a black pouch around her neck and tipped the porters. A dollar would have sufficed but I put it down to excitement. Norman looked dapper in his favourite khaki trousers and veldskoen shoes, clutching a duty-free packet of red wine. They both looked tired.

"When is Christianne coming, darling?" Pattie asked, mid-hug.

On the drive home, I described the houseboat and various islands and bays we had planned to visit on the Lake. Norman asked about the fishing at this time of year and was surprised that I'd not found out what engines powered the houseboat. Pattie marvelled at the Jacaranda trees in early bloom and noted that the zebras in the Mukuvisi woodlands, matched her skirt. My parents were back in Zimbabwe, and our home would be filled with family again.

"When is Christianne coming?" Pattie asked again.

****

28

During the political violence of the last disputed election, Hildah had been beaten badly and her small home and cotton crop in Mount Darwin were burnt to the ground. When a good Samaritan brought her through to A&E in Harare, all she had left were the bloodied clothes on her back and a national identity card sewn into her petticoat for safe keeping. 22 years earlier she had been Vicki's cousin's childminder and Vicki rushed to her aid when she heard about the incident. As it so happened, Jules and I were looking for a housekeeper and Hildah thought it was a blessing straight from above when she moved into our two-bedroomed domestic quarters and started work three months later after her bones had healed.

"God is there!" she ululated, raising her hands in the air.

She immediately assumed the role of Minister of Home Affairs and made sure the house and its occupants were in good working order. She loved our animals just as much as we did, and it was not uncommon to see her lobbing a toy to Muffin or teasing the cats with a blade of grass. Both our cats were SPCA rescues; Mac, was a squint ginger tabby, and Nyimo Bean, a tiny cream Heinz 57. Hildah made sure fresh milk and biscuits were laid out for them all throughout the day.

Scruffy had a tenuous relationship with her, both were broken from abuse, and both vied for my attention. He would accept food from her but that was it. Hildah constantly tried to make friends and because of his poor vision, ensured that all the household furniture stayed in the same place so he could get around easily.

When I arrived home from work, all five of them usually stampeded into the car park to be the first to greet me. The ululation from Hildah, squealing from Muffin, barking from Scruffy and meowing from the cats always made for a warm, noisy welcome.

To prevent Scruffy bumping around the car park I always picked him up first. He could smile at me and growl at Hildah at the same time, just to remind her it was his home first. She never reacted and offered plenty of reassurance to stop him from barking at her.

"Stop it, Scruffy. It's me, Hildah," she told him.

With Scruffy under one arm, I'd lob a toy for Muffin, stroke the cats and ready myself for a bombardment of information from Hildah as I walked through the front door.

"Madam, the generator needs diesel. Madam, a branch of the avocado tree has fallen. Madam, the tap in the kitchen is leaking. Madam, did you remember dog food?"

The first item that she bought with her wages was a bright green apostolic church uniform to replace the one that had gone up in smoke during her assault. We bought her a bicycle on which to ride to church and she proudly presented herself at the kitchen back door. Scruffy lost his voice, barking at the green blur with wheels and a bell which Hildah pinged frequently with delight while still trying to reassure him who she was.

"Stop it, Scruffy. It's me, Hildah, and I'm going to Church," she informed him

Scruffy didn't care if she was going to Mars. I had to put him in the study for a while just so I could ululate with Hildah and God about her fresh new garb.

One evening, Hildah made sure that she won the race to the car door so she could tell tales on Scruffy before I melted with his smile.

"Madam, Scruffy doesn't want me to do the washing."

Quite how a tiny dog had stopped her from doing it would be an interesting story. As it turned out, he was hiding amongst our dirty laundry during a thunderstorm and wouldn't let Hildah anywhere near it. I picked him up from the floor and despite his smile, gave him a stern talking to for not letting Hildah do her chores. Satisfied with the telling off, Hildah marched down the passageway to collect the laundry!

Hildah had only just got over the excitement of Colleen and Noreen arriving when she was informed of Pattie and Norman's impromptu visit. Carpets were hoovered again, every glitterstone floor tile and wooden carving were re-polished. Cupboards were dusted several times over, windows sparkled, and brass doorknobs gleamed. Our entire household dazzled in preparation for the arrival of mdala[22] boss and mdala madam.

When Pattie and Norman came through the front door, they greeted Hildah like long-lost friends. It was a friendship forged from numerous lengthy telephone conversations about my well-being.

"God is there!" she exclaimed, holding Pattie's hand.

Scruffy was beyond terror when Pattie walked towards him with her crutches reverberating on the stone tiles.

"Gosh, darling, doesn't he look like Ringo Star?" she commented.

They met Colleen and Noreen for the first time and soon enough the whole house was alive with chatter. Hildah proudly presented a tray of tea with Pattie's favourite ginger biscuits on the side. Muffin took advantage of all the visitors and plonked her toy onto every lap and the cats swirled their tails around every leg. Colleen and Noreen discussed their

---

22. Shona word for old.

work as Royal Ballet teachers and discovered they had many friends in common with Pattie in Zimbabwe's theatre world.

It wasn't long after tea that Norman took himself upstairs to bed. Pattie became anxious and followed him up shortly afterwards, looking distracted. It was ten o' clock in the morning, but they'd had a long flight. When I checked in on them a few hours later, Pattie was pressing a bathroom towel down on the carpet with her crutches and Norman was squeezing out another one in the shower. I'd forgotten to mention that it was important to close the taps even if water didn't come out of them, which was usually the case when the generator was cooling for an hour every four hours. While they were sleeping the generator had kicked back on and water flowed from the tap that they'd left open, flooding their bathroom and bedroom. Hildah rushed upstairs with a bucket and mop with Scruffy snapping at her heels. Jules and I pulled every towel from the linen cupboard and pressed them into the carpets. Norman was embarrassed and Pattie was distraught.

"I don't know what happened, darling!" She said shakily.

"It's only water Mum, I should've warned you." I replied.

It was the first of many floods during their stay.

Christianne arrived with Scott and Benjamin a few days later. The boys immediately threw off their clothes and plopped into the swimming pool, unaccustomed to the African heat. Pattie took them on adventure walks around the park and came back with pods, seeds, and insects in a plastic bag tied to one of her crutches. There was great excitement showing us all the creatures that they had never seen before.

In the evening, we whisked Christianne off to Avondale Club for a reunion with all our friends. We returned home later than expected and a little under the weather. As I opened the front door, a river of freezing water splashed down the steps, followed by a packet of toilet rolls. The basin taps of the downstairs toilet spluttered, having emptied nearly five thousand litres of water from the storage tank onto the floor. Jules squealed as the rubber toilet mat took the shape of a stingray and knocked at her ankle. Scruffy and Muffin barked from the stairs, unwilling to wade through the cold water to reach us.

"Shoosh," I whispered to them, as Jules and Christianne mimed exaggerated swimming strokes around the kitchen floor.

"You two get the mops and the broom. I'll check on Mum and Norman." I ordered.

They were fast asleep, unaware of the tsunami below. The clean-up took hours and our sense of humour lasted half that. In the morning, I hid every basin plug in the telephone drawer. Hildah asked how mdala boss was going to shave without one, but I didn't care, the whole house stank from the damp. Only after spotting Norman stuffing the plughole with a flannel, did I issue him with one plug only!

We had sundowners and snacks around the veranda bar the night before the houseboat trip. Norman clutched onto his favourite Bollinger beer and was deep in conversation with Colleen and Noreen. Ben was playing on a rubber tube in the swimming pool and Scott hurled the toy for Muffin from the edge. Christianne was sunbathing on a deck chair with a glass of wine by her feet. Norman and Pattie were delighted when Vicki popped in to say a quick hello and were glad to hear that she and Julie would be joining us on the boat. It was a beautiful warm August evening, but Pattie started to get fidgety when Vicki asked what time we planned to set off in the morning.

"Not five hours beforehand, like the ferry trip, I hope, my Lovebug," said Norman, lovingly grabbing her hand.

Pattie looked questioningly at him and didn't find the

comment funny at all. I changed the subject and suggested that she exchanged some of her sterling for the more accepted US dollar. She emptied her black pouch on the bar counter and had one thousand pounds in twenty-pound notes around her neck!

"How much do I have, darling?" she asked.

"Mum, you shouldn't carry so much money around with you!" I exclaimed.

"Ok, darling, but how much is there?"

I thought she was confused about the exchange rates, but she kept re-counting the fifty individual notes, one, two, three and so on. She no longer seemed to understand the value of money and couldn't multiply. I recounted the notes out loud with her; twenty, forty, sixty and so on. She put five notes back in her pouch for the houseboat trip and handed over twenty notes to Vicki to exchange for US dollars. I put the balance in the safe upstairs and when I returned, Pattie was having a complete meltdown and all conversation had stopped.

"Who has taken my money?" she demanded, staring at the reduced number of notes in her pouch.

"Mum, I've put the rest in the safe," I replied.

"No, no!" she shouted, "Norman's taken it!"

Christianne rushed in from her deck chair when she heard the words.

"He hasn't, Mum. You gave twenty notes to Vicki and the balance is in the safe," I reiterated.

"You! How could you?" She accused Vicki.

Pattie demanded that Norman empty his wallet.

"Oh, my Lovebug!" he pleaded.

It was so out of character that we were left stunned and embarrassed. I rushed upstairs to the safe and handed her back the money, hoping to quell the situation. Pattie jammed it back into her black pouch and asked when dinner would be served before going upstairs for a quick recount in the quiet of her bedroom.

From that moment on she hid her jewellery and make-up bag under the mattress. After locking the bedroom door, she wanted to phone her bank in England to get more money. Despite crying down the phone, the telehandler refused to release her funds because she couldn't remember the telebanking password, which was a relief.

I decided that it was in her best interest to swap the fifty 20-twenty-pound notes with fifty worthless billion-dollar Zimbabwe notes, which I did secretly when she was in the shower. It was the first time I'd deceived my mother and I felt sick to my stomach. Norman's heart sank when I told him where the sterling was hidden if he needed it and he agreed to book Pattie a doctor's appointment as soon as they got back to England. I had a sleepless night imagining brain tumours and the like and didn't know then that this turned out to be the first significant incident in my mother's battle with Alzheimer's disease.

****

29

We decided to separate Norman and Vicki from Pattie on the journey. She remained guarded towards them both and happily got into my car with Colleen, Jules, Noreen, and Scott. Norman, Christianne, Ben, and Julie travelled with Vicki in her twin cab. The five-hour journey flew by and each landmark that we passed triggered a clear and colourful memory of Pattie's filming career, in stark contrast to her confusion over the money.

"Gosh look!' she exclaimed when we reached the town of Banket. "Those are the Ayrshire Hills. I brought the girls here in a military convoy during the war. We had a broomstick out the window!" She giggled.

Her articulate, humorous narratives captivated Colleen and Noreen. Each of their questions received an embellished, accurate response. I held my breath when Pattie paused in conversation to recount her money. She didn't react to the change of currency which was both a relief and a concern.

Scott and Ben had never been to Kariba before, nor had they been on a houseboat. The 20-metre twin decked pontoon provided the boys with a myriad of places to explore. We had specifically chosen the boat because it was child friendly and they ran around like monkeys, exploring all the nooks and crannies with Christianne in pursuit with a bottle of sunblock. She lathered it on when she captured them at the boat wheel where the captain gave them turns to steer us out of harbour.

Colleen and Noreen settled into their cabin on one side

of the boat, overjoyed at the simple luxury and fulfilment of a lifelong dream. Pattie and Norman were in the second ensuite cabin. While they unpacked and freshened up the rest of us got comfortable on the upper deck which had a dining table and chairs, a bar, sun loungers and a splash pool.

I was initially concerned how Pattie would manage the steep steel stairs on her crutches; one slip would've been deadly. But, with years of practice, she understood her own limitations and stepped onto the top deck with fresh make-up on, wearing a blue floral cotton dress and a large bush hat.

"Hello, darlings. Isn't this lovely?" she squealed at the view.

The journey across the lake to Palm Bay would take five hours and, not long after we set off, Julie presented a magnificent array of cold meats, home-made pickles, salads, and French bread. She had become quite the foodie in recent years. At the lunch table Colleen was struggling with the sun on her face and accepted Pattie's offer to borrow a hat. Within seconds of placing the hat on her head Pattie became uneasy and snatched it back.

"That's mine!" she scowled.

Colleen apologised but Pattie left the table, making a harrowing descent downstairs and returned with all her hats on her head!

"Mum, do you know you've got three hats on?" Christianne cackled at the absurdity.

"Well of course I do, darling," she answered, unfazed.

Embarrassed, I suggested a game of Boggle, which had become a family favourite. Pattie found plenty of words and spelt them correctly but paid no attention to the rules. When the timer ran out, she had a half-page of words but didn't cancel matching words out with the other players and won every game as a result. We all sensed something was amiss but for some reason, let her get on with it.

"Gran, you're the Boggle Champion," said Ben.

"That's good, darling," she answered.

The sun was going down by the time we reached Palm Bay. It was a beautiful evening but too late to take the tender boats out and go fishing or on a game cruise. We settled with sundowners and snacks on the top deck around the splash pool, but we were all in bed early after a long day.

At first light, we took Ben and Scott out on the tender boats to go fishing. They saw crocodiles and hippos for the first time, but the fishing was dreadful. We were back at the houseboat by ten for brunch by which time Norman had surfaced and both he and Pattie were leaning over the balcony waving us in. Wearing her three hats, Pattie shouted down to us trying to find out what fish we had caught and started to giggle when Vicki raised a small kapenta[23] fish in the air. It was about 7 centimetres long which Vicki felt took a huge amount of skill to foul hook.

"Oh dear, never mind darling, come upstairs for a cup of tea, it fixes everything you know," Pattie giggled.

By the time we got upstairs everyone was laughing at Vicki's antics with her tiny fish, including her attempts to cut it into 11, minute slithers for us to have for lunch!

"Gran, we saw crocodiles!" Scott shouted.

"Lovely darling, did you hear the lions and hyenas last night? She asked.

Those of us who had slept out in the open on the top deck had spent a very noisy night listening to lions fighting over their kill and chasing away hyenas that were on the scavenge. In the morning we could see marabou storks and white-backed vultures landing on the carrion of an impala which the lions had killed.

We moved to a new bay each day after brunch and it was

---

23. A freshwater sardine.

the perfect time to chat, play games, snooze or read. Pattie used to read a lot, but I noticed that she didn't pick up a book. She preferred to stare out at the water or recount the money in her black pouch.

Every evening, after a series of careful manoeuvres, we got her on board one of the tender boats for a game cruise. The elephants and impalas on the shoreline piqued her interest and sparked more stories of her adventures.

"Remember the elephant in Ruckomechi camp, Lissie?" She giggled.

Traditional sing-a-longs followed every evening meal, and everyone took turns choosing a favourite song. Norman sang his Dulwich school song, which impressed Colleen and Noreen who, by the third verse, joined in with *"Quotquot"* this and *"Quotquot"* that. It was like the good old days and Ben and Scott thought the older generation were slightly loopy. We had to prompt Pattie to think of a song but after starting her off with one of her favourites, *"We Aint Got a Barrel of Money"* she continued with the remaining verses. It spurred her on to sing *"Non je ne regrette rien"*, which was a shame, and she received an encore from everyone except Christianne and me!

The fishing was great on our last day. Scott and Ben caught their first tiger fish and Noreen caught her first bream, which were both moments to treasure. The bream fishing was so good that Colleen suggested we have fish and chips for dinner which everyone bar Pattie agreed to. She was glaring suspiciously at Colleen who had borrowed Jules' hat and was too distracted by it to answer!

Colleen and Noreen said it was the best holiday they had ever had. Apart from a couple of odd moments with Pattie, it was a fabulous trip, and she improved each day with further rest, maybe that's what she needed. But on the drive back to Harare her demeanour changed completely. She didn't recall any stories and was anxious about time, worried about the three hats on her head and frantic about Norman.

"Where's Norman?"

"He's in the car in front, with Vicki." I pointed out.

"Okay, darling but where's Norman?"

By the time we reached Makuti an hour later, my patience had worn through.

"Darling, where's Norman?" she asked again.

"Mum, we left him on a milestone," I snapped.

Colleen tapped me on the back of the head from behind for my rudeness.

"Why is he there, darling?" she asked in turmoil. "Stop, stop, where's Norman?" she shouted, trying to open the car door. Central locking saved her.

By the time we stopped for tea at Lions Den, the tension could've burst through the windows. I suggested we put Pattie in the car with Norman to allay her fears, but she refused and got back into my car.

"Darling, where's Norman?"

From the moment Christianne, Scott and Ben left to go back to England, Pattie became unsettled. I arranged a farewell afternoon tea and received several questioning glances about some of her behaviour. But her joy was obvious when Margaret and her son James arrived with his wife Sarah, followed by her cameraman, Willie, and his wife, Gabby. Nicky - Pattie's friend whose house burnt down - turned up after a few toots at book club. She handed Jules a plate of snacks which had nothing other than a paper placemat in the middle! The cheese scones had gone AWOL enroute and Nicky appeared not to have noticed. Jules thanked her anyway. Was everyone going mad?

Janis and Charmaine also arrived with Sam, their Amazon Green parrot. One squawk from the creature sent Scruffy into hiding. Muffin thought it was a toy and tried to snatch it for her own and Sam took flight into a tree. Pattie tried to tease the bird onto one of her crutches and shrieked when he moved even higher. Eventually, Charmaine shimmied up the tree and got him down.

On the day of their departure, Pattie was dressed in her zebra print skirt again. She had packed her suitcase but refused to let it out of her sight. She wouldn't let anyone bring it into the lounge and sat on the stairs with it where we joined her for tea, like it was the most normal thing to do.

"When are we going?" she asked anyone.

Eventually, we left an hour early to soothe her anxiety. Norman gave Colleen and Noreen an enormous hug and squeezed Jules and me so tightly I thought we'd burst. He looked rested and promised to book a doctor's appointment for Pattie. Some form of medicine would surely sort this out. Pattie wobbled straight to the car following her suitcase and didn't look back at the smiley faces waving goodbye.

****

30

She made a terrible fuss about going to the doctor until Norman lost his temper with her for the first time ever and forced the issue. She was instantly referred for a CAT scan at Bournemouth Hospital, but the referral letter never arrived.

"Mister, I have had a lifetime of being poked and prodded by doctors, I'm not going," she argued.

In the meantime, I received a few emails from her, describing visits to the Heavy Horse Park and Stonehenge with her grandchildren. But it was not long after this that her correspondence became one-line statements, telling us how much she loved and missed her children. Christianne and I spoke daily about our concerns but, until we had a diagnosis, didn't know what else to do.

Norman also started answering the landline, which was highly unusual. He made excuses that Pattie was in the shower or down the passage somewhere. When I asked about the CAT scan, he said they had still not received a letter, but Pattie had been getting to the post first. He sounded subdued and explained that he'd had his first car accident in over 70 years of driving. It happened when he took Pattie on another adventure to Burley in the pouring rain and he misjudged an island, burst the front tyre, and was inconsolable about the mistake. Something was not right. Vicki and Lisa agreed to oversee the paint business, Hildah relished the thought of being left in charge of our home and Jules and I booked tickets for the first available flight over.

We arrived during the *Big Freeze* of 2010. Major airlines

were grounded because of heavy snow, except for Air Zimbabwe. I held Jules' hand for most of the flight and didn't sleep a wink listening for the engines and waiting for some aerodynamic ice issue to cause the plane to drop out of the sky!

Through the snowfall I could just about make out that Pattie was waving at us from the foyer, but her greeting was flippant when she opened the door.

"Where have you been?" she implored.

She was dragging her right leg more than usual and gave me a curious look when I told her how much I had missed her. We met Norman in the passageway on the way up to their flat. He was pulling a trolley of clothes towards the in-house laundry and looked haggard but gave us an enormous welcome.

"Liza, my back has been giving me trouble," he revealed, as Jules took over the chore.

Pattie had forgotten the last load of washing in the laundry for three days. When he enquired where it was, she returned with someone else's clothes.

"Darling, can you get Mum out of her zebra print skirt? She's not been out of it since we got back from Zimbabwe."

He washed, spun-dried and hung the skirt back behind the bathroom door every day, so it was fresh for her each morning.

Nothing had changed in the spare room except the usual welcoming packets of Jelly Baby sweets were missing. Pattie immediately became unsettled when my suitcase of gifts and treats disturbed the room.

"We need food, let's go, darlings!" she said, fiddling with the black pouch around her neck.

Norman sighed and reached for the car keys.

"Mum, I'll take you, but can we have a cup of tea first, it been a long trip?" I replied in an attempt at normality.

She approached the kettle cautiously then side-stepped towards the hoover and started vacuuming the carpets. Above the noise Norman explained that she cleaned day and night and no longer did any cooking. He'd been ordering ready-made meals.

"I hope you enjoy sausage and mash; I've ordered four for tonight," he shouted.

With the hoovering complete, Pattie buffed the cushions, adjusted the casual throws, and recounted the fifty billion-dollar Zimbabwe notes in the black pouch. I could see several twenty-pound notes had crept back into it.

"Let's go, darlings!" she demanded.

The snow-covered ground outside looked formidable; it was not the time to be going out in the car, but Pattie was standing at the door. We returned from the shops in one piece with enough food for an army, and enough choc o pains for a navy! While she packed the food away in strange places, I asked Norman why he hadn't told us how much worse Pattie had got.

"I never want to be without her," he replied, with tears in his blue eyes. "They will separate us, and I promised never to leave her."

We cried together, but agreed we needed help. I phoned the doctor for a duplicate CAT scan referral and booked it for two days' time. In the few hours we had been with them, Jules and I were exhausted - something more than a cup of tea would be needed to fix this.

The hoovering started at 5am the next morning and droned on for an hour, after which Pattie locked herself in the bathroom. An hour later she was still in there and I needed the toilet, but she wouldn't let me in, despite my pleas. In desperation, I peed in a bucket in the utility room. She nonchalantly emerged wearing the zebra print skirt.

"Hello, darling," she said, without a care in the world.

I locked myself in the bathroom and turned on the shower to hide my investigation. The cabinet was filled with plastic bottles of medication. Incorrect dosages could be the cause of her behavioural change. Three bottles of liquid morphine were on the shelf and, after reading the prescription, I resolved to keep an eye on the level of the open bottle and hid the two others in the linen cupboard. I also removed the lock from the bathroom door.

Pattie laid out the knives, forks and condiments on the breakfast table and listened to the news on television which was so loud that I developed an instant frown. Norman said both their hearing aids were missing but mercifully I found the television remote control and hit the mute button. Pattie retreated to their room and was packing away trinkets when I flopped on her bed to chat. She eyeballed me when I moved a pillow under my head but contributed to the conversation as I told news of Zimbabwe.

"This is my holy communion crucifix and chain," she remarked, giving it a kiss.

"Oh, look, darling, here they are!" She said, delighted.

She had found Norman's hearing aids and tried to insert them into her ears. When they didn't fit, she popped them back into a trinket box. Dying inside, I walked through to tell Norman where to find them.

"Mum, have you written your Christmas cards yet?" I asked to change the subject.

She didn't respond. It was December 15th, by this time of the year her walls would usually be plastered with Christmas cards that she received in response to the hundreds she sent out. Family and friends would find it highly unusual not to hear from her over the festive season and I didn't want to raise the alarm. After sneaking out to Morrisons to buy several packs of cards and stamps, I laid them out on her desk, but she had no idea where to start.

"Let's do the cards for family and close friends first, I'll post them tonight and we can hand-deliver the rest to your friends in the complex," I suggested.

I opened the precious A4 file marked *Pattie's Address Book* and it was empty, bar a scribbled piece of paper with her name, national insurance number, and a list of her allergies. A lifetime of contacts had disappeared.

"Who should we send these to?" she asked.

Luckily, Christianne could help with the addresses of family and close friends. She was just as shocked to hear that the address book no longer existed. Pattie didn't know what to do when I opened the first card for her to write.

"Darling, what shall I say?" she asked.

"Dear Mags, Chris, Elizabeth, and James," I started.

Her spelling was as good as it was in the game of Boggle on the houseboat, but she only wrote what I spoke and nothing more. Norman helped name the friends at their complex and, once their cards were written out, Pattie and I took to the passageways to deliver them as I read out each name.

"Oh, June! I know her. Come on, darling, let's go," said Pattie.

June lived diagonally opposite but didn't invite us in having lost patience with Pattie's incessant visits. We knocked on almost every door along both sides of the passageway and anyone who answered was greeted with a warm smile from Pattie. Some joined in the Christmas spirit and gracefully accepted a card from strangers, others slammed their doors. I was embarrassed, angry and sad all at the same time, couldn't they see that my mother was trying her best.

"Mum, where does Sally live?" I asked, gruffly.

"Over here!" she shouted beetling towards a corner flat.

The woman refused to take the card. She wasn't Sally! With the commotion, a white-haired man wearing a vest, opened his door and greeted Pattie with a huge hug and a kiss. I was relieved at the recognition.

"Allo, love. Aw right then?" he shouted in a cockney accent.

"Hello, Jim," Pattie replied coyly.

I explained we were delivering Christmas cards but flicking through the pile realised we didn't have one for him.

"Sorry," I lied, "We must have left yours in the flat; I'll pop it in later."

When I started to cry at the hopelessness of the task, Pattie became uptight and turned on the speed, dragging her leg behind. No matter how much I implored, she wouldn't stop or slow down until the last card was delivered. I eventually hid a pile in my waist band just to get it over with and calm her down.

"We're finished, Mum," I lied again. "Let's go home."

When she fell asleep next to her trinkets, I got the correct names and flat numbers from June and posted the others in the post box at the top of the road. Pattie was awake and counting her money when I returned and announced that she needed to go to the bank to get some more.

"Haven't you got enough in your black pouch, Mum?" I asked.

Norman stirred from his seat in front of the television, the volume down ten notches having retrieved his hearing aids from the trinket box. I told him to stay where he was but mentioned to Pattie that she needed to wear something a bit smarter than her zebra print skirt to go to the bank in Ringwood.

"Let's choose something lovely, Mum," I suggested.

She became uneasy when I pulled out a dress from her cupboard.

"No, not that one!" she said, stuffing it back on the rack.

"You have such beautiful clothes Mum. What about this skirt? It'll go with your polo-neck sweater, red hat and red gloves," I persisted.

Pattie stroked the fabric of the floral gypsy style skirt.

"Ok, darling." She popped it on and patted a red beret onto

her head.

"How do I look?" she asked.

"As beautiful as ever," I replied.

While we were out, Norman hid the zebra print skirt at the back of the wardrobe and put an end to Pattie's fixation with it.

Bank staff greeted her with smiles and waves, and she was directed to the front of the queue because she was on crutches.

"How much do you need today, Pattie?" asked the youthful, well-groomed teller.

"How much do you think I need?" she asked politely.

I stepped in and asked for twenty pounds in five-pound notes, remembering it was the quantity, not the value that Pattie found crucial. She couldn't remember her PIN, so the teller wrote out a withdrawal slip, which she managed to sign, before stuffing the cash into her black pouch.

We met the bank manager on the way out and I asked if we could have a quick chat. He took us into a client room, but Pattie did not engage with him, she was more interested in counting out her wads of cash out loud onto the table. "One, two, three." The problem was obvious to the manager, and he agreed to set a twenty-pound limit in small denominations on daily withdrawals. When he leant in for a closer look at the fascinating billion-dollar Zimbabwe notes on the table, Pattie snatched them away giving him the evil eye. As a diversion, I produced a 100 trillion-dollar note that I kept in my wallet as a talking point. He managed a quick glance at it before that was snatched that away as well!

****

31

Above the drone of the hoover, I suggested to Pattie that we go on a trip to find the New Forest ponies and have a pub lunch afterwards. I didn't mention the CAT scan appointment beforehand and dreaded her realisation of my deceit. She packed the hoover away pronto and within minutes was ready and dressed in the same gypsy skirt outfit as yesterday.

Norman had always been slow to start in the morning. His routine was stubbornly methodical, and he was already in a state about hiding the appointment from Lovebug. Today of all days I needed him to hurry so we could get the ordeal over with. After twenty minutes waiting in the car with Pattie and Jules, I stormed back upstairs to find out what was taking him so long.

He was in the bedroom half-dressed, trying to re-attach one of his braces to his trousers with an elastic band.

"Liza, one of the clasps has broken," he sighed.

My heart sank at the sight of him in a holey vest struggling to tie a simple knot, his fingers too big for such an intricate task. My mother had been so much my focus, that I had neglected him.

"Where's Norman?" Pattie said, having walked back upstairs to find us.

I tied the clasp to his belt loop with three elastic knots, buttoned up his shirt, threw a coat over his shoulders and pushed him out the door, promising to stop and buy new vests and braces before we went to lunch.

Once the engine started and the doors were locked, there was no turning back. Norman keyed in the postcode for the hospital on his new satnav but couldn't figure out how to turn the volume up. With pressure to get going, he started to drive and by the time we reached the highway the volume was up to its maximum.

"Prepare to do a U turn!"

He had pressed the home button instead of the start button, which was all we needed.

"Prepare to do a U turn!"

"No, no," Pattie argued, reaching for the map book.

During her debate with the satnav, I slipped in that we were going to the hospital for her scan before lunch.

"I'm not going," she said, defiantly.

"You're in the car, Mum. We are going!" I said forcefully.

"Prepare to do a U turn!"

"Darling, why must I go?" she pleaded, tearfully.

"Mum, it's a simple scan to check why you are forgetting things."

"Prepare to do a U turn!"

Jules pointed out a signpost to the hospital, but we missed the turning.

"I'm not going. I won't forget, darling," she cried, pulling at the door handle.

"Prepare to do a U -turn!"

"Can you look in the map book and find the route for us, Mum?"

"Oh, alright, darling, which hospital?"

Her role as chief navigator had kicked in and diverted her thoughts.

"Prepare to do a U turn!"

"No, no," Pattie argued again, "throw it out the window! Go off the next exit, I know how to get there."

Norman hadn't yet learnt how to change a route setting on

the satnav which sounded exasperated by his disobedience. I leant over from the back seat and disconnected it, just so we could all think. In doing so we had to trust Pattie's navigation, and after going down a few interesting roads arrived at the hospital car park just in time.

It was a long walk to the X-ray department, and I put Pattie in the only available wheelchair. Walking arm and arm, Jules supported Norman along the passageways, stopping frequently so he could catch his breath. At this rate we were going to be late, so I sped ahead with Pattie and bomb shelled the quiet waiting room. Pattie pushed the swinging doors open with her crutches, making a superstar's entrance and giving everyone an enormous smile, which made them nervous. After settling her down with a magazine on the Royal family I went to check her in while Norman and Jules caught us up. He walked straight to the toilet within the waiting area and was in there for such a long time that I knocked on the door.

"Norman, are you alright?" I whispered.

I could feel the stares on the back of my head.

"Where's Norman?" Pattie shouted.

"I'm in here, darling," he boomed, flinging the toilet door open.

He emerged with his shirt unbuttoned and braces trailing on the floor.

"Liza, the elastic's gone again," he chuckled.

Pushing him back, I squeezed into the room with him, and we both started to laugh.

"Where's Norman?" Pattie yelled.

Banging on the door, Norman threw back his head and roared with laughter, releasing all the pent-up tension of the morning.

"I'm indisposed, my Lovebug," he bellowed, wiping away tears of laughter from his cheeks.

"Norman, breathe in. It's too tight. I can't stretch the elastic enough to tie it," I giggled.

"I am breathing in," he replied, heaving with laughter.

"Stop laughing! I can't tie it with your stomach moving."

"Darling, I can't stop."

"Fewer pints for you today, Mister," I said, giving his trousers a good yank.

"I'll need new braces before lunch, to keep it all in," he cackled.

"Can we get you out of the toilet first? On the count of three, breathe in!"

We emerged from the tiny room looking red faced and sideways glances at each other set us off laughing again. By now the entire waiting room looked uncomfortable. Pattie added to their discomfort by waving a hand in the air showing off her favourite ring, admitting that it had come from a Christmas cracker that she'd opened on the QT! The waiting room was relieved when we were called through for the scan and I left Norman with strict instructions not to breathe, for fear of another burst-out!

The brain scan went surprisingly smoothly, Pattie chatted all the way through it, and I resolved not to be so deceitful with her going forward.

"I've had many of these for my hips," she informed the radiologist.

At lunch, Pattie pointed out the New Forest ponies that she could see through the pub window and with his new braces on, Norman ordered a pint of beer with confidence. I realised quickly that Pattie couldn't comprehend the words on the menu, which explained why she had dumped her address book. Looking at the pictures she selected the roast beef special but when it arrived said it was not hers and wanted my plate of spaghetti bolognaise instead. Checking his notes, the waiter apologised, but I gestured for him not to worry and swapped plates.

I drove us home via the hardware store in Ringwood so that Norman could buy a fuel filter for his car. As he hobbled off with Jules and disappeared into the shop, Pattie started to get anxious.

"Where's Norman, darling?" She asked.

"In that shop, Mum, buying a filter."

"Oh, darling, but where is he?"

I tried to distract her by talking about the New Forest ponies, but it did no good. Norman would be taking his time, telling some poor unsuspecting teller everything there was to know about combustion engines.

"Where is Norman? Let's go!" she demanded, with a wild look in her eyes.

"He's buying a filter, Mum!" I roared.

I was horrified when she opened the car door and got out into the road to look for him. I'd forgotten to put the central locking on and was about to abandon the car and give chase when Norman and Jules appeared.

Norman had arranged to spend Christmas in Kent with his son Clive, but the weather was worsening, and I expressed my concerns about them being on the road by themselves. Pattie had already packed her suitcase and refused to consider going by train, which was how I intended to get up to Christianne for Christmas day and how Jules planned to go to Farnborough to be with Colleen. It was so strange being in England and not spending Christmas with my parents.

On our last night, Pattie went to bed early. Norman made her a noisy cup of Milo, whisking the hot milk with a fork to make it frothy which was the way she liked it. I heard him give her an enormous smooch on the lips as he handed it over.

"Goodnight, my Lovebug," he said.

"Goodnight, Mister," she replied.

We sat up with him for a few drinks, savouring the opportunity for normal conversation. I made one final check on the oral morphine in the bathroom cabinet and let Norman know that Pattie wasn't taking any as the level hadn't moved. After showing him where I had hidden the other bottles, we caught up on news from home. He asked about Vicki, Julie, Janis and Charmaine and returned from refilling his wine glass carrying a worn-out brown leather suitcase with his special letters, photographs and accomplishments inside. With a twinkle in his eye, he pulled out a photograph of a water pump that he'd engineered and installed in a dam in Mutoko. He showed me his long service award from Triple Jay Engineering and a picture of him leaning proudly against his doomed *you know what* that went into the Ewanrigg River. Jules was shown the press cutting of his home-grown 92-kilogramme pumpkin that won him the runner-up trophy and he remembered how awful it had been having to eat it all.

"Waste not want not!" he remarked, reminding us of one of Pattie's favourite sayings.

The new African record was a massive 149-kilogramme pumpkin, and we chuckled at the thought of how that family must have suffered ploughing their way through it. He raised a photograph of his mother and remembered his brother, Les, fondly. I looked at his enormous hands, which had frightened my teenage boyfriends but couldn't tie an elastic band.

"I only stopped playing wicketkeeper at the age of 53 you know," he said, proudly. "You and Christianne spent many long days at Stragglers Cricket Club watching my games," he added, taking another gulp of wine.

"Darling, what is going to happen to Mum? I promised I would never leave her, but I'm 90 next year!" he blurted out.

"Whatever happens we will look after you both but

promise me you won't hide anything from me again," I pleaded.

I could see the relief in his eyes as they welled up.

We said goodbye at the flat door to avoid Pattie getting anxious. She gave me a kiss on the cheek and after spotting my suitcase, scurried off to check her own.

"Goodbye Liza." Norman said, giving me a kiss and a bear hug. Jules got the same.

"You've got room for a few more pints with those new braces, and stop worrying, ok, we'll sort everything out?" I smiled.

"Splendid, darling, splendid," he replied.

Jules and I waited around the corner from the complex for a bus to take us to the train station, not realising they were on half service due to the snow. Ordinarily, we would have walked back to the flat for a large mug of tea and made another plan, but I didn't want to confuse matters for Pattie or face another goodbye. I was so close and yet so far from them. We boarded a bus three hours later, frozen to the core.

The weather worsened the next day and news reports advised against any road travel. Norman cancelled their trip; both he and Clive were relieved, but Christianne and I were miserable that they'd be spending Christmas on their own eating a ready-made meal. We remembered the priceless family gatherings with Norman dressed up as Father Christmas, handing out presents and glasses of sherry while Pattie cooked up a storm.

We arrived back in Zimbabwe on New Year's Day and what we did next would depend on the CAT scan results. In the meantime, the supplier of ready-made meals had been given a long-term contract, an account had been opened at the local launderette with collection and delivery, cash withdrawals had been limited, the zebra print skirt was hidden, and Norman had peace of mind.

****

32

He died 10 days later. Both Vicki and I broke down and sobbed at the paint shop when my brother Stephen phoned with the news. Christianne raced down to Dorset and learned that Pattie had lain with Mister's body the entire night before looking for help. He would have loved that.

I hid under the cabin blanket for most of the flight. Jovial holiday makers in the adjacent seats made it difficult for me to listen out for the 737 engines which I expected to fail at any minute. Norman always found my fear of flying irrational and I tried to remember his lengthy explanation on the "splendidly" engineered CFM56-7B turbo engines, but it was no use. At thirteen thousand feet in the air, his soul could have brushed past me. Perhaps my last conversation with him allowed him to go peacefully in his sleep. The thought prompted a muffled meltdown under the blanket which exploded when a startled air hostess innocently offered me chicken or beef.

"Eat? My dad has just died!" I blurted out.

Pattie was not in the foyer to greet me; the flat door was open, and I found her making space in her trinket boxes for the new additions of Norman's wedding ring and wristwatch. She greeted my sadness with a detached coolness which made me question whether she fully understood what had happened. I hoped the vociferous drone from the hoover would drown out her usual repetitive question "where's Norman?" but she never mentioned his name again.

I found a will in his brown leather suitcase, which took

precedence over the power of attorney that we had and gave my mother full authority over his estate. Without having received a diagnosis of her condition, she was considered capable and of sound mind, which she was not. It was a fine example of how gaps develop in estate planning. We should've had a lasting power of attorney for both of their health, welfare, property, and financial affairs. It would've made matters simpler. Fortunately, the bank manager remembered me from our last visit and transferred funds to the funeral parlour so we could get on with the arrangements.

Well-wishers made the flat untidy, Pattie barely interacted and mostly scowled at them from behind the exhausted hoover. Christianne selected favourite hymns and passages from the Bible, and I handed Pattie the final layout of the Order of Service. She kissed Norman's picture on the front page then tore it up. I was unsure whether she disliked the design or whether that was her way of saying goodbye. Without saying a word, she toddled to her desk and opened her A4 address book. On the tattered piece of paper listing her allergies and national insurance number she added the line *my husband has died*. The meagre eulogy acknowledging Norman's death was a relief and it was the last grammatical phrase she ever wrote.

Norman was cremated in Poole on January 24th. His son, Clive, grandson Brendon and granddaughter Charlene read poems and passages from the Bible; his daughter, Mandy, flew in from Australia and read the eulogy. Stephen and his family caught the ferry from Ireland and James flew in from Zimbabwe to represent Margaret. Colleen and Noreen drove in from Farnborough and my friend, Simon, from my horse-riding days, was a sight to behold. The church was crammed with family and friends from Zimbabwe and around the globe. Mark's family lay a cricket bat on his coffin. We asked the congregation to sing loudly, as Norman would have done.

Many had experienced a rendition of *Quotquot annos, quotquot menses*, and understood what was required.

The wake was held in the reception room at their complex and celebrated the life of a fine man and loving husband. Simon and I made a lethal punch which spurred on outbursts of Norman's favourite songs and hilarious memories of his many antics. Pattie was surrounded by her children and grandchildren enjoying the impromptu family reunion. I wasn't sure whether she fully understood what was happening as she didn't cry but she was impressed with all the condolence cards and delighted by all the flowers.

When it was all over and Pattie and I were alone in the flat, I experienced what Norman went through in the last days of his life and was unprepared. Pattie laid the table every morning with Norman's favourite breakfast of muesli, apple and yoghurt for me to eat. The only time I had a break from the hoover was when we went out on drives, but we had to back in time to receive the delivery of ready-made meals. I poured a noisy mug of Milo every night as Pattie's separation anxiety with Norman disappeared and was directed fully at me. She followed me everywhere. The bathroom door was flung open when I was on the loo or in the shower, conversations and phone calls were interrupted and when she wasn't near me, I worried where she was. It was exhausting.

"Where's Lissie?" she constantly asked.

With lack of sleep, frustration, and the constant drone of the hoover, I lost my temper easily and cried a lot which made Pattie anxious and scared. It was impossible to sort out their affairs and look after my mother at the same time. I needed help. When I phoned Pat, my ex-office manager, who'd been repatriated to Swindon years earlier, she caught the first bus down. Her arrival was my saving grace, and I broke down and sobbed when she appeared at the front door. Pattie and

Pat knew each other previously and had enjoyed each other's company, but in my mother's mind our new visitor had made me cry and because of that she was instantly suspicious of her, which made me cry even more.

"Why are you crying? It was me who loved him," Pattie snapped.

"Of course, you did, Mum, me too," I sobbed.

What made matters worse was that I needed Pat to be my accomplice to help pack up Norman's belongings. I'd already been in England a month and with my return flight looming and a new paint contract starting, it needed to be done with ruthless speed. Pat was reticent but understood my predicament and we quietly cried about it out of Pattie's view. Bar a few special possessions for his children, most of his belongings would go to charity. Of course it was too soon, but Pattie couldn't make decisions, nor could she fetch, carry, or drive. Each time we laid out his clothes, she put them back in the cupboard which was heart-breaking. I gave Norman's new braces a sniff and popped them into my suitcase, hiding my tears. It was a strange memento, but it worked for me.

"What are you doing with those?" Pattie asked, pointing at the Dulwich School, Harare Men's Club, and Stragglers Cricket Club neckties.

"These should go to Clive; he would love them, Mum."

"Okay, darling," she said, hanging them back in the cupboard.

Norman's clothes see-sawed from black bags to rack and back again. I lay with her every night after dinner and explained our next steps while she drank Milo and examined her trinkets. Once she was asleep, we quietly filled the plastic bags.

Pattie threw the neurology referral letter into the bin without opening it. I retrieved it when she wasn't looking and booked the appointment to see a specialist in Poole.

Sitting in the reception area I recognised the haggard signs of another daughter struggling to answer her mother's repetitive question, over and over again.

Pattie's diagnosis of Alzheimer's disease was in black and white. The damage to her brain so far was irreversible, but a new drug could slow deterioration by about two years - with no guarantees. It was a lifeline offering nothing but time.

"Can you still cook, my dear?" he asked.

"Yes, of course," Pattie answered.

My pupils enlarged and I shook my head to indicate she could not.

"What about driving?" he asked.

"Absolutely." She gleefully recalled whacking the sump driving through a riverbed in Africa.

The specialist ticked a lot of boxes. I couldn't fathom why he took her answers when he was the one who'd diagnosed her with a brain disease.

"How long has my mother got to live?" I whispered to him with tears welling.

"This is not a natural ageing process. It is a disease of the brain. They say Alzheimer's descends on sufferers like a thick white fog, initially a mist that dulls the senses becoming thicker and thicker. It happens fast with some and slower with others. You will need a care package for her and to get this you need to book a health assessment. Look out for urine infections," he advised, tearing off a prescription note.

Feeling nauseous, I booked the assessment immediately and after explaining my looming departure they arrived the next day to begin. A sympathetic health worker informed me that it was their mission to keep Britain's elderly independent for as long as possible. I liked the idea, Pattie loved her flat and from the way it was being explained, the correct care plan would enable her to remain there. Perhaps my blinkers were on, but all of this was new to me and if the medicine stopped any further degeneration for a year or two, all I had to do for now was to make sure functions that Pattie couldn't perform were substituted by something or someone else. I was dumbfounded to be told the assessment would take six weeks - I could tell them instantly what she was capable of and what she needed.

Pat returned to Swindon before the health workers arrived. Pattie was glad to see her go, but she would never understand what it meant having my friend there during such a tough time.

During the first week of the assessment, I handed out copies of the diagnosis like junk mail. Christianne applied for a court of protection/lost capability order over Pattie - but approval could take time. The local pharmacy agreed to deliver a weekly pill box for the health workers to administer during their twice-daily visits. They arrived at six in the morning to make sure Pattie was dressed and took her medicines with a cup of tea during breakfast. At 6pm, they were back to heat the ready-made meal and administer more medicine with a cup of Milo. The schedule was tiring, but at least the days were free for adventures in the car. The pattern quickly became familiar and by the second week, I opened the door for them in my pyjamas.

I lay on Pattie's bed one evening and decided to explain Alzheimer's disease to her, as best I could, and told her that when I left to go back to Zimbabwe the health workers would help her with all the tasks that she struggled with.

"Will I be alright, darling?" she asked.

"We will make sure you are, Mum."

"Where's Lissie?" she asked.

By the third week, the health workers decided that Pattie needed more care and lunchtime visits were included in the schedule. This restricted the length of our adventures in the car and instantly changed Pattie's opinion of them.

She started to get up at 4am to dress and to clean the flat in the hope of reducing their number of visits. By the fourth week, she locked the front door, and lost the key, which led to many conversations with them through the keyhole. When I suggested a trip in the car, the keys miraculously appeared.

"I don't like those girls," she exclaimed.

"Mum, they are trying to help," I snapped.

"Ok, darling," she replied, toddling off to fetch the hoover.

By the fifth week, Pattie saw them as mortal enemies and stuck one-worded messages on the front door saying *Gone* or *Away*. When this failed to deter them, she wedged objects against the door. I could see she was unhappy but had been told that it was best for Alzheimer's sufferers to remain in their familiar environment and had a key safe installed outside the front door for ease of access.

My packed suitcase made Pattie anxious, so I hid it in the laundry.

"I don't want to stay here," she announced.

I lay with her on my last night and explained that we would move her to be nearer Christianne but that would take a few weeks. In the meantime, she needed to listen to the carers and let them look after her. I believed that everything was in place, to keep my mother safe and well and slipped out of the flat unnoticed while she was distracted by lunch with my brother, Mark, and his boys. The health workers would be in by the time he left and would get her ready for the night. The care support package would kick in after that.

Two weeks later, the matron gave Christianne notice to remove our mother from the complex. Pattie had become a public nuisance and was at risk living alone in the flat. She had been found down the road trying to hand over Norman's gold wristwatch to a stranger. Fortunately, the good Samaritan recognised the signs and walked her back to the complex. Christianne collected Pattie the next day and telephoned the removals. Transferring Pattie's social care and benefits from Dorset to Suffolk County Council would take around two months and included a new six-week assessment. The last assessment still had wet ink.

Christianne's eldest son, Joshua, agreed to look after his grandmother while the transfer was being sorted out. He adored her and it worked well until one afternoon, Pattie crept out of the house and Joshua ran outside just in time to catch a glimpse of her red glove boarding the bus to Colchester.

"Hello, darling." Pattie waved at him from down the bus aisle.

My siblings and I had differing opinions about bringing Pattie back to Zimbabwe. After the last failed attempt at independent living in Dorset, it was more than likely that her new care assessment would recommend she be put in a home, and I couldn't bear the thought of that.

Jules and I had just moved into a larger property and felt Pattie would be happy and safe with us. Our Minister of Home Affairs was sure to keep on top of things when we went to work, and Pattie could wander around the walled garden as much as she wanted. We also had the love and support of our friends to call on for help if needed and firmly believed that love would conquer all. Christianne's husband, Graham, bravely agreed to escort Pattie back to Zimbabwe and our simple lives prepared for the impending storm.

****

33

I had an hour to kill before the airport run and poured a large mug of tea to drink on the veranda and gather my thoughts. The heavy-duty walker that I'd hired was tucked into a corner ready for Pattie to use. It would be far safer than her crutches on the uneven glitterstone floor tiles. I put my full body weight down on the handles to test its sturdiness again and Muffin jumped into the front basket with a toy, wanting a ride. I pushed her around the furniture on another test drive and envisaged her and Pattie going on lovely adventures along the garden paths together. Scruffy wouldn't go near it and took off each time its wheels squeaked on Hildah's perfectly polished tiles.

With the knowledge of past experiences and more Alzheimer's research, I felt confident that we would cope better than I did in England. I'd had some rest and the paint business was back on track with a new office manager. The excitement of seeing my mother again outweighed any bad memories of my previous struggles with her. Pattie had lost her husband and home, had moved to a new county – albeit briefly – and was about to land in another country. Tough for any 81-year-old, let alone one with a mental disorder.

Hildah was excited to see mdala madam again and made sure the spare room off the passageway was immaculate. She had been briefed on what to expect with the illness.

"It doesn't matter Madam; she is your mother," she said.

We had piled familiar objects into Pattie's room. A signed copy of her book was placed on the bedside table and a painting of guinea fowls by David was relocated from the lounge and put above her bed. Family pictures dotted the side walls, and a duplicate photograph of Pattie and the Pope was hung above the dressing table. A welcoming bouquet of handpicked garden flowers sat on the dressing table but the packet of Jelly Babies on her pillow had gone missing.

"Madam, Muffin's stolen it," Hildah snitched.

Muffin kept all her favourite toys and treasures in a nest under the bed in Pattie's new room. She collected anything round, fluffy, crackly or squeaky and the packet of Jelly Babies never had a chance of reaching my mother's lips. Her room of treasures was rarely disturbed, and she was flustered by all the activity around it.

Graham pushed Pattie out of the airport in a wheelchair, they both looked exhausted. Pattie was wearing her floral gypsy skirt, polo neck sweater, red gloves, and a large bush hat. The strings from the black pouch around her neck tangled with her crutches as she waved them in the air.

"Let's go!" She shouted as I took a deep breath.

I could tell on the drive home that she'd deteriorated in the month since I'd seen her. She was more anxious, and her sentences were truncated, but she noticed the giraffes within the fence of the Mukuvisi Woodlands. I dared not point out the zebras in the adjacent field in case it sparked memories of the skirt that Norman had hidden. She waved at the tomato vendors and women grilling maize on wood fires at the roadsides but couldn't describe them. She recognized Harare Drive, Nazareth House Church, Borrowdale Road, and Sam Levy's Village but couldn't put a name to them.

"Gosh ...there's what's it?" she muddled.

Our entire household rushed out the door to greet us. Mac and Nyimo swirled their tails around Graham's heels as he marched towards our veranda bar to recover from the flight. Jules received an enormous greeting from Pattie and Hildah raised her hands in the air shouting out "God is there!" Scruffy snapped at her ankles but smiled when Pattie leaned down to stroke him, until the tick of the dreaded crutches sent him off into hiding again.

I led Pattie down the passageway to her bedroom and she became anxious when I opened her suitcase, eyeballing me closely as I hung her clothes in the cupboard. Christianne had packed clothes for every occasion and three months' worth of medicine was locked away immediately. Nyimo flopped onto the suitcase flap and purred, Mac meowed when Hildah arrived with a tray of tea, ginger biscuits and a saucer of milk for the animals. Muffin leapt up onto the bed and nicked a woollen hat with a large pom-pom from the suitcase to add to her treasures under the bed.

"Stop, stop!" Pattie shouted at Jules, who was on all fours, trying to get it back.

Once the pom-pom hat had been returned and the suitcase emptied, Pattie stood up and marched down the passageway.

"Let's go!" She growled, pushing the heavy-duty walker aside.

"You look worn out, Mum," I said, following her to the lounge, "don't you want a lovely hot bath?"

She turned back down the passageway and locked her bedroom door, stuffing the key into her black pouch. After noticing that there were keys in all the other doors, she took them as well. Christianne had warned me that Pattie was fixated with keys, but I didn't anticipate experiencing it from the get-go. Only once every key in the house was in her possession, did she agree to have a bath and was asleep not long afterwards. A cool gentle breeze flowed through her bedroom windows and carried the beautiful sound of a Heuglin's robin. She looked peaceful and safe. I returned the keys to each door while she slept and joined Jules and Graham at our bar to commiserate his horrendous flight.

Our first day with Pattie hadn't been bad at all.

At 4am the next morning, she banged her crutches on the door and barged into our bedroom.

"Let's go, darling!" she said, with a naughty smile, her crutches armed in a double-barrelled shotgun position.

"Ok, Mum. Let me get changed first." I said dashing to the bathroom.

She plonked herself down next to Jules and began rummaging through the bedside drawer taking whatever caught her eye. Moving on to Jules' wardrobe, she grabbed several items of clothing that appealed and popped them over what she was wearing. Muffin peeped out from under the covers and eyed a fluffy scarf that had been dropped in the scrummage.

"Where's Lissie?" Pattie shouted.

"I'm in the loo, Mum."

The separation anxiety with me had returned and she barged in.

"Hello, darling."

"Morning, Mum. Won't you be hot with all those clothes on?"

She peeled a few layers off and hung them in her bedroom cupboard.

"Let's go!" she said.

After a quick cup of tea and some toast, we were in the car by 7am, taking a leisurely drive down Crowhill Road and past her beloved Esher Close. She pointed out the substantial double storey houses that were being built on her favourite view that was once cabbage and wheat fields.

"Gosh, look!" She shrieked.

Although she couldn't verbalise it, she had always been against the development of a golfing estate in the area and years ago had submitted several petitions to the local council.

Within minutes of returning home, she spied the door

keys again and locked Graham and Jules in their rooms as they slept. It took some convincing to get them back and release the angry inmates from their cells. From then on, every door key was put on the top of the door frame, out of reach.

I left for the paint shop feeling that Pattie would be safe and content with a busy day ahead. Margaret was visiting at 10 o' clock for tea, Julie was popping in at 3pm and Vicki was arriving for sundowners, but Hildah phoned me at lunchtime in despair. Pattie had cunningly used her crutches to slide the keys off the door frame and had locked herself into our bedroom with Scruffy. Hildah was in the garden talking to me on her mobile phone while pleading with mdala madam through the bedroom windows. I could hear Scruffy attacking the windows each time she leant in to speak.

"Madam you have the keys. Look in your bag. Stop it, Scruffy, it's me Hildah!"

By the time I got home they'd been locked in for two hours and both were desperate.

"Help, help!" Pattie banged the windows with her crutches, sending Scruffy to the ensuite shower.

"Mum, hand me your bag," I implored.

She wouldn't relinquish her black pouch and just as my mobile phone connected to the locksmith, Pattie produced the keys.

"Gosh, let's go!" She pouted, unlocking the bedroom door, and scuttling off.

Every key was removed from each door and locked in Hildah's house for safekeeping from then on.

At one o'clock the next morning I heard ticking down the passageway. One of the crutches had already lost its rubber stopper on the glitterstone tiles and clicked like a toothache. The dogs barked at the strange sound in the middle of the night and woke the house. Pattie was fully dressed in her floral gypsy skirt, suede jacket, knee-high leather boots with a bush hat plonked on her head.

"Are you alright, Mum?" I grumbled.

"It's time for church," she announced.

"It's one in the morning, go back to bed"

"Let's go. Quick!" She yelled.

After a cup of Milo and the promise of church on another day, I guided her back to the bedroom, but she was adamant. I shouted, begged, pleaded and sobbed in desperation. It went on for two hours.

"Don't you want to go to bed?" I asked, dead on my feet.

"Yes, ok, darling." She said, lying back against the continental pillows, fully dressed.

After hours of giving her angry commands, she responded instantly to my passive, exhausted tone. It was a revelation and I covered her with the duvet when she finally shut her eyes but dared not remove her boots in case it woke her up.

The following night, Scruffy heard Pattie's crutches ticking down the passageway towards our bedroom and he threw back his head and howled. I cursed myself for forgetting to buy a rubber stopper and stormed towards the door before Pattie had a chance to bang on it.

"Oh, hello, darling. Your hair's nice. Want a brush?" She said, waving a nail brush in the air.

"Yes, Mum, but can we go to bed afterwards?" I said in a passive tone.

"Okay," she replied, gently brushing my hair.

Events of a similar nature occurred each night and it didn't take long for the strain to show. After a weepy visit to the doctor, fortification came in the form of Zopiclone for sleep and Bromazepam for anxiety – for all of us!

The drugs added a couple more peaceful hours of sleep to the night, but not enough. Pattie put herself to bed early and the drugs wore off by the midnight hours, when she was sprightly, needy, and I was comatose. She often woke me up from a drug-induced coma, with a poke in the ribs with her crutches.

"Let's go, darling!" she whispered from my bedside.

I started to lock the bedroom door at night, which led to frenzied rattling of the door handle. If this didn't evoke a response, a door bashing followed. Jules and I started tiptoeing around the house to remain undetected for a little while at least. We left for work earlier than usual, where mistakes were made and stayed on after closing time. Hildah was constantly gentle and caring, Jules was subdued, I was haggard and sharp.

Pattie's friends visited but most only came once, after struggling with her state of mind, so I called in the troops who all knew that a ride in the car settled Pattie down. Charmaine set Pattie's hair once a week and took her on a drive afterwards, Julie popped in for tea as much as possible and a road-trip followed. Vicki took Pattie to church and Delia took her for haircuts. She was content in the car, but we couldn't be in it around the clock. The daytime was manageable; it was the nights that were killing us. We needed more help!

I cried through our first meeting with Jan Wood of the Zimbabwe Alzheimer's and Related Disorders Association (ZARDA). Jules explained events while I sobbed and desperately listened out for solutions to improve the situation at home. Jan confirmed that it was sleep deprivation that affected caregivers the most. Respite was vital to cope with the daily challenges of the disease. She asked if Pattie could be moved anywhere to give us a break and to get more sleep. When I mentioned our small cottage at the bottom of the garden, she thought that it might be the perfect solution.

"How do we get her to go there?" I asked.

"She is still intelligent. Speak to her honestly and emphasize the positives. Although the muscle of the brain dies with Alzheimer's, what you have already learnt in life is still in there somewhere."

It was a beautiful April morning. Purple-crested louries chattered noisily from the palmtops and turtledoves cooed from the bottlebrush trees. With newfound hope and courage, I walked Pattie through the garden with the animals, inching towards the thatched cottage.

"Gosh, look!" Pattie smiled.

"You could live there if you want Mum," I said casually.

I explained how she could make it her own, have her own privacy, own garden, visitors, anything! Piling on the positives I added that Hildah could stay with her at night and during the day she could come across to the main house.

"This is beautiful, Madam, God is there!" Hildah contributed.

"Let's go…quick, quickers!" Pattie said, turning away.

I thought our plan had failed but as we reached the swimming pool, she swivelled round on her crutches.

"Back, back!" She shouted.

Hildah looked up to the heavens and raised her hands silently into the air.

The contents of Pattie's old room were moved to the cottage while she was out on a drive with Vicki. The small lounge was rearranged into a bedsit and the double bed positioned against a wall near the bathroom for convenience. A welcoming packet of Jelly Babies was placed on the kitchen counter out of Muffin's reach. Favourite pictures were hastily hung on the walls and a few African carvings were scattered around the fireplace. Jules arranged garden flowers in a bowl and put it on the TV counter next to the ginger biscuit tin. We hung a spare set of curtains on the lounge windows, they were a little short but would do for now. My only concern was the wooden staircase to the loft, and we decided to lace rope across the entrance to prevent access. By the time Pattie got back, the cottage looked like it had been lived in for years.

After eating a cottage pie dinner together, I handed her several family letters as a distraction. International post took an inordinate amount of time to arrive in Harare, so I'd asked family and friends to send emails instead. I put them into envelopes addressed to Pattie and she was delighted to receive any form of correspondence. She read intermittent words out loud before stuffing them into a leather handbag that she'd taken from Jules' cupboard and carried the excess from her overburdened black pouch. I kissed her goodnight and snuck out while she was admiring drawings from her grandchildren with Hildah.

Jules and I had our first full night's sleep since my mother's arrival. I felt rested and rushed over to the cottage to find out how Pattie had spent the night. The TV was on and Lukwesa Burak was reading the news. Hildah was doing the washing up and Pattie was sitting on her bed, paging through her letters, with a cup of tea and ginger biscuits on the side drawer. Scruffy, Muffin, and the cats had already snuggled up on her duvet and were listening intently to the gobbledygook family news that Pattie was reading out to them.

Hildah reported that before going to bed she'd read passages from the bible to mdala madam who had only got up once in the night for the toilet.

"Oh, hello, darling," Pattie said indifferently.

"Morning, Mum. What are you reading?"

It spurred on a re-examination of her letters while I made a thick oats porridge for breakfast. Hildah left to get ready for her day and was back in time for me to leave for the paint shop. I anticipated a bad reaction from Pattie, but she was shuffling through her handbag and barely lifted her head when I said goodbye. This was going to work!

****

34

Pattie's first week in the cottage worked well and with more sleep, Jules and I coped better with the daily challenges that Alzheimer's disease presented. But at the start of the second week, Minister of Home Affairs telephoned me at work to report that Graham had left the house angry and had walked to Sam Levy's Village, just to get away.

"Mdala madam shupas[24] him all the time," she said.

Graham was only meant to stay for a week but his return flight to England had been cancelled due to an industrial strike and the first available booking with a different airline was in two weeks' time. I was unaware that when I left for work Pattie beelined for the main house and woke him up each morning by bashing his bedroom door with her crutches and he'd had enough. Wearing nothing other than his boxer shorts, he flung the door open, directed a few choice expletives at his mother-in-law before stomping off to the shower. Pattie followed him there and banged on that door until Hildah created a diversion by calling her through to the kitchen for tea, giving Graham a chance to escape.

Hildah also reported that she hadn't been able to complete the housework. Not because of Scruffy this time, but because caring for my mother was a full-time job and she was falling behind in her chores. However, "God was there" because her friend from church was available to do care work and her presence would keep mdala madam busy, boss Graham

---

24. Shona word for agitate.

happy and allow the housework to be finished. She phoned me back a while later to say that she had spoken to Catherine who could come for an interview at 5pm. Boss Graham had also returned in a much happier mood - she thought it might be because he had been drinking beer!

He had given mdala madam a three-pack of lipstick as an apology for his earlier language. Pattie had crammed it into her leather bag without saying a word to him. She was distracted by our electrician who'd arrived to replace the inverter batteries. Before he could turn off his car engine, she'd plonked herself down on his front passenger seat and refused to move. He phoned me in a panic, and I suggested that he drive her around the block. Fortunately, on his return Delia had arrived to take her to the hairdresser.

"Why?" Pattie questioned.

"To make you look pretty," Delia shouted from her car window.

With that, Pattie jumped ship and pulled down the sun visor in Delia's car, looked into the vanity mirror and applied a double coat of new lipstick before bursting into song.

"I feel pretty, oh so pretty."

Delia joined in by adding the next line "I feel pretty and witty and gay." The singing continued throughout the journey and into the hair appointment, where a few bemused clients with hair in rollers, were cajoled into singing a verse or two!

When I walked into the cottage after work, Catherine was on the edge of Pattie's bed, cackling at her own attempt to sing "I feel pretty." Pattie had applied a thick layer of red lipstick onto both Hildah's and Catherine's pouting lips.

"Here's your post, Mum," I said casually.

While I examined Catherine's CV, Pattie studied the emails from my brothers several times over, shouting out the occasional word. Catherine listened enthusiastically to the gobbledygook that Pattie was speaking and commented on every identifiable word that she heard. It was enough of an interview for me, and I employed her on the spot.

Vicki organised a farewell braai for Graham when his departure date was eventually confirmed. Emily, from the days of rhino capture in Rukomechi camp, arrived with her daughter, Beth, as did Delia, Janis, and Charmaine, and my recorder-playing friend, Noreen. We sat on the veranda in the warm sun, reminiscing and Pattie was the centre of attention, but silent moments spoke volumes of her obvious decline and inability to interact. When lunch was served, she wolfed it down, tossed the plate aside and had a complete meltdown.

"Please, please, help me, help me, let's go, quick!" she screamed.

I rushed to her side, but she was hysterical and nothing I said calmed her down. I couldn't understand why she was suddenly so utterly distressed. Was she in pain or was she frightened because she couldn't recall the stories or the people we were talking about? She couldn't tell me what was wrong. I knew that large groups increased confusion for Alzheimer's sufferers, but we were hardly a noisy horde. I put her in the car and beelined for A&E, but her demeanour changed instantly, and I decided against taking her to the emergency rooms. We drove home via the Umwinsidale Hills where she pointed out the beautiful Tibouchina trees lining the roads and sighed at the piles of rubbish at the bus stops we passed.

"There's no such thing as rubbish!" She shouted, tapping the car window. "Help!"

After the incident at Graham's braai, the word 'help' never left my mother's vocabulary, and I was constantly reproached by angry strangers coming to her rescue when she called it out.

Catherine settled in quickly and we developed a schedule that worked well for all of us. Pattie enjoyed her company, and the beautiful garden walks that they went on three times a day. Catherine went off duty at 5pm when I arrived with Pattie's dinner, and then Hildah took over from me at 7pm for the night. I returned in the morning and made breakfast before leaving for work when Catherine arrived for the day shift.

Dinner with Pattie was our quiet time together. I handed over newspapers and letters and told her my news of the day in one-sided conversations, while she ate. When she was full, she pushed the leftovers into the middle of the plate, wiped down the knife and fork with a napkin and put them back on either side of the place mat ready for the next sitting. She was contributing to the housekeeping and Hildah knew to wash them properly later. After dinner Pattie flicked through the newspapers while I made her a noisy cup of Milo and handed out her medicine. She never liked taking the pills and often purposely dropped them onto the floor and flicked them under the bed with her crutches. When I produced another pill, she pretended to choke when she swallowed it. Bathing and changing her into her pyjamas were simple tasks but getting her dentures in or out was another story altogether. A glass of denture cleaner fizzed on the side drawer in preparation for the activity.

"I don't have any," Pattie argued, tapping her front teeth to prove it.

"You do, Mum. They need a scrub, don't they?"

"Help!" she yelled.

Having not owned a pair, I found it difficult to demonstrate and we both gagged when I tried to pull them out for her. Eventually she would get on with it, but we had the same battle every morning and evening.

"Mum, where are your teeth?"

"I don't have any," she smiled.

Her choppers were frequently lost or squirrelled away in a variety of hidey holes. I would often find them in the biscuit tin, wrapped up in a handkerchief with her rosary and Norman's hearing aid. I learnt that anything foreign to the body becomes exactly that to a person with Alzheimer's disease.

On one occasion she categorically refused to take them out and after an hour of trying I gave up and let her sleep with them in but booked a dentist appointment for the following afternoon. I thought it would be difficult keeping her still in the chair, but the dentist's gentle manner and fascinating dickey tie kept her calm. He slipped them out easily and pointed out an area of roughness causing abrasion on her gums. Was this the cause of her breakdown at Graham's farewell? She looked relieved to have them out. The rough area was filed down, and the dentures were cleaned and polished, but as the dentist leant in to insert them, she snatched them back and gave them a kiss.

"I love you!" she told her sparkling choppers, before popping them back in.

After two months as Pattie's carer, Catherine started to limp. Pattie wanted more frequent walks, and the daily mileage was putting a strain on Catherine's knee.

"Madam walks plenty round and round the garden," she said.

I bought them both doodle art pads and colouring-in books to make sure they rested more, neither were impressed. Folding the laundry was a far more satisfactory task which on one occasion included the cotton table napkins. Pattie instantly became fixated with them and refused to relinquish them from that day on. She sat for ages folding and refolding the pile on her lap, which was of no bother to anyone and kept her off her feet. Unpicking the hem to lengthen the cottage curtains also kept them stationary for a few days. I got home to find them both on the pool loungers in the sun surrounded by crimson bougainvillea and vermilion poinsettias. The shrill call of the Heuglin's robin was trying to out-sing a Laughing dove. Pattie was draped in curtains and the dogs and cats were nestled in the overflow at her feet. It was an idyllic scene, until she saw me and dropped everything, except the napkins.

"Help! Quick, quickers!" She cried.

For no apparent reason, she was suddenly on the verge of another meltdown. We went for a drive to Domboshawa Hills, past the broken remains of Hatcliffe Squatter camp where her soup kitchen had been and where she had discovered David. We passed my old horse-riding school and Helensvale garage, where Julie and I had queued for fuel on horseback. Pattie was unmoved at the sight of them, her Alzheimer's had gone to another level and she was going to need professional care soon.

Catherine resigned a month later; her knee simply couldn't keep up. Modiester replaced her and Pattie took an instant dislike to her when she arrived at the cottage wearing nurse whites bringing back fears of the health workers in Dorset. Her opinion however, changed the next day when Modiester arrived in civvies, pushing a wheelchair that I'd hired to get my mother off her feet. Pattie's face lit up at the thought of having her own wheels.

Modiester started taking her outside the property onto the sideroads where the wheelchair was easier to push and where Pattie would see more than the four perimeter walls of our home. They became regular features wheeling down Borrowdale Road on another adventure, making friends enroute. They met a Rastafarian tomato vendor whose children gathered around the wheelchair out of curiosity to watch table napkins being folded and to examine a set of dentures that Pattie had handed over to their father as a gift. I made it clear to Modiester that she should take back anything that was given away.

Each day Pattie wanted to go further and further from the house. On one occasion our neighbour spotted them several kilometres away and stopped to see if they were alright. Before Modiester could answer Pattie leapt from the wheelchair into his sports car with a pile of table napkins, shouting for help. Modiester gave him quick instructions to drive back to our gate while she ran after them with the wheelchair which wouldn't fit into the boot of his sports car. She lasted just over a month before complaining of a sore back. The wheelchair had already had four blowouts!

When the third nurse, Patience, arrived, nothing would settle Pattie and her separation anxiety with me returned with vengeance. She shadowed me to the vegetable garden, round the pool, to the bath and to the toilet. Sensing my desperation, she became more desperate herself and was no longer happy in her little cottage, banging on our bedroom window at all hours, screaming for help. Windows were broken and during moments of lucidity she was terrified.

I came home early from work one day to find her on the kerb outside the house, screaming for help. She was in a worse state than the episode at Graham's farewell because Patience had refused to take her down Harare Drive again in the wheelchair. Wild-eyed, Pattie stood up shouting for help and tottered when her table napkins dropped to the floor. Patience grabbed her arm to steady her, and Pattie recoiled with such vehemence that she teetered backwards near a deep French drain. I caught her just in time, the fall would have killed her. Pattie was hysterical until I got her into the car and took her on another drive. Patience resigned the next day and we struggled to find another nurse able to cope with the physical and mental demands of looking after my mother.

Hildah also had to go back to her tribal lands for a few weeks to look after her own unwell mother. With no respite, I was on the edge and lost my temper easily. Pattie sped around the garden nonstop on her crutches, driving me crazy. Despite the addition of a light morning sedative, she wouldn't sit for more than a minute unless she was in the wheelchair or the car, where the frenetic folding of table napkins reached new heights. She watched movies for seconds, the news for less. When I cooked a meal, she trudged through the kitchen, out the back door and around to the cottage, again and again. Each time we met in the kitchen she asked where I was.

"Where's Lissie? Help!"

"Mum, have some tea and biscuits."

She took a quick gulp of tea before going on another circuit around the house and garden. I didn't know how to stop her, and it made me angry seeing her legs dragging more and more each day. When breakfast was ready, she sat for a few minutes but became anxious waiting for the toast to pop up.

"Quickly. Help!"

"Mum, I can't go any quicker," I stupidly argued, "here fold some more napkins."

"Ok, darling… quickly, help!" she replied, agitated.

"Stop saying quickly," I barked in frustration.

"Ok, darling, quick, quick, quickers," she said, cleverly changing the word ending.

She ate the breakfast ferociously and again pushed her leftovers into the middle of the plate, wiping down the knife and fork before setting off again.

Jules reminded me to be careful with my tones and moods. Alzheimer's sufferers see mirror images and react accordingly, but I couldn't help myself. I cried with frustration, which frightened Pattie. She cried, I sobbed because I made her cry, and dashed to my room, furious at my lack of control. Within minutes of blowing my nose, Pattie found me again.

"Where's Lissie? Help!"

"I'm here. Sorry, Mum, let's go for a ride."

"Quickers, darling, quickers," she repeated as I opened the car door.

If the telephone rang while she was passing by on her rounds, she answered it politely then slammed it down.

"Who was on the phone, Mum?"

"Maureen," she answered with a smile, then cried.

Her sister Maureen had died 22 years ago, but the telephone call upset her, and she plonked herself down onto the wheelchair, rocking its tattered wheels into motion, wanting another ride. "Quickers."

Conversations became whispers, I tiptoed around the house more and more and even hid behind curtains to avoid Pattie seeing me. It was pathetic, desperate behaviour towards someone I loved. I couldn't wait for the couple of hours respite on Sundays when Vicki took Pattie to church.

"Try St George's Mass, Vix; she loves the boys' choir."

The Catholic Mass would be familiar but lengthy and ten minutes into the service Pattie started to fidget. By the time the congregation got up to receive Holy Communion she was screaming out for help. The following week Vicki decided that her own Pentecostal church might be a better option. It had a shorter service with a live band and jubilant music to keep Pattie occupied. When the Pastor announced the lamb raffle results, Pattie waved her crutches in the air and shouted out "lambs to the slaughter, help!" It was the last time my mother attended Mass.

"She's changed!" Pattie said, pointing at Vicki and clapping her hands in the air.

It was astute of her to notice that Vicki had become a born-again Christian, but with Pattie no longer attending Mass, my only form of respite was gone. I was broken and sobbed down the phone explaining to Christianne that I couldn't cope and was sending our mother back to England. When I told Pattie our plans, all she understood was that she was going somewhere and marched around the garden trying to get out, shouting for help.

Our friends Fiona and Claire understood the care system and completed Pattie's registration with Suffolk County Council in record time on our behalf. I booked my mother on the earliest flight back and sobbed with relief and gratitude when Vicki instantly agreed to escort her there. Our last week together was dreadful as I wrestled with my guilt and desperate mirror images reflected on my mother creating more anxiety and fear for her. I should've been wrapping my arms around her, singing her to sleep with the *"Mountains of Mourn,"* or *"Mighty like a Rose,"* not secretly packing her suitcase and counting the hours. I wouldn't look at myself in the same way ever again. Christianne was determined to make it work this time around and felt as I once did, that love would conquer all.

****

35

It was a beautiful September morning, and I was sitting at our veranda bar waiting for Christianne's weekly Skype call with Pattie. With every gust of wind Jacaranda flowers rained down into the swimming pool and Hildah was fighting a losing battle, skimming the floating carpet of purple blooms off the surface with a leaf scoop. Muffin was leapfrogging with grasshoppers on the lawn and Scruffy was on my lap nervously waiting for the next clatter of dates to fall from the palms and ricochet off the aluminium veranda roof. A Heuglin's robin was bathing in a puddle on the pathway leading to the bottom of the garden where fluffy red bottlebrush flowers abseiled down the roof of Pattie's empty cottage. It was her 85th birthday and she had been in a home for Alzheimer's sufferers for four years. I stared at the duplicate photograph of her with Pope John Paul II, which had made its way to our veranda bar for all to see. For four years I have fought with God, as pieces of my mother's personality disappeared for good. Four years since I had written anything in this book.

My heart skipped a beat when I answered the call and Pattie's face appeared on the screen. She was slumped in a chair but perked up a bit when she saw me. Or maybe it was the picture of herself on the bottom of the screen, or Scruffy? She opened her mouth as Christianne fed her a Jelly Baby and laid a newspaper on her lap.

"Happy birthday, my darling Mum!" I shouted. "Look,

here's Scruffy."

She didn't react, she was fixated on a photograph of Queen Elizabeth II on the front page of the newspaper.

"When last was she checked for a urine infection?" I asked Christianne.

"'Yesterday. They are giving her antibiotics. I've bought her a sweater for her birthday, but her clothes get mixed up here. She's wearing someone else's slippers."

Christianne whistled to Scruffy, and he barked in recognition. Pattie said something gobbledygook and, seconds later was fast asleep, hugging her favourite Snoopy toy. That was her birthday. I said goodbye before tears flowed and phoned Vicki immediately, hoping her faith could give me the answers why my devout mother had to suffer so.

"This is a man-made disease. God didn't want this for her," she answered.

A few weeks later, Pattie started having seizures which we expected as the disease took complete hold. She was found on the floor in the passageway, motionless and they kept her in hospital overnight for observation. Christianne arrived to find her in a wheelchair in a glass room with a panic button twisted around the arm rest. Did they expect Pattie to press the button for help, ask for a drink or to go to the toilet?

"She's got Alzheimer's!" Christianne roared.

Pattie walked half a step the next morning and because she could weight-bear, was sent home. A few hours later, the ambulance was called back to the home. A black lump was visible on the top of her right leg and an X-ray revealed a break in three places. One break was so severe it was at right angles, practically through the skin.

"She can't tell you where it hurts!" Christianne exclaimed. "Has she been given a drink, does anyone around here understand anything about Alzheimer's?"

There was very little training offered on the disease at the time. The doctor called the orthopaedic surgeon, who dosed her up with morphine and asked us to consider the Alexander Effect. The operation would remove the entire leg from the hip joint.

I frantically gathered information to make the right decision. If she had the Alexander Effect she wouldn't walk again, which might be a blessing. Could they put a fifth hip joint in? How would we keep her still while the bone healed? My mind boggled and then it hit me that the only reason Pattie went through all the previous operations was to remain on her feet. That was my answer, no matter how ridiculous it sounded. I phoned the hospital as it opened in the morning to authorise any operation that would save her leg, but she was already in surgery!

"What are they doing to her?" I seethed.

"I can't say, but it was an emergency," said the nurse.

A nurse at Kate Middleton's maternity ward had committed suicide after a telephone prank call to King Edward VII's Hospital. As a result, telephonic information was barred.

"This is not a hoax; I am her daughter, phoning from Zimbabwe."

No matter what I said, I couldn't get any information and cursed the two Australian perpetrators for broadcasting the prank.

"Why was I not contacted? Who signed the consent form? What if I needed to say goodbye?"

Seven nail-biting hours later, I got the news that Pattie had come through the operation. They'd put a pin down her donated femur and wired the broken bones to it. She wouldn't be able to weight-bear for a month, but would walk eventually, if she remembered how to.

I caught the earliest flight to London, Pattie's leftover Zopiclone helped me manage the journey on my own. She had spent 10 days in hospital, and I held back my tears and shock when I first entered the respite home and a faint odour of detergent stuck to the walls.

Residents babbled to themselves in chairs, while others roamed the corridors, yakking to no-one. Pattie sat in an orthopaedic chair that Christianne had organised. She looked frail, and mumbled something when she saw me, her voice was still hoarse from the anaesthetic.

Each day I sat with her for hours in the 'quiet room' telling her stories from home and rubbing her hands which were arthritic from holding crutches for 30 years. I read out the completed family tree, which she had started to research before she got sick. I needed her to know one of her ambitions had been fulfilled. She rustled the papers around staring at the photographs of relatives glued next to each name. Staff members stopped and listened, intrigued with my stories about Pattie's life in Africa. Henry, a fellow resident, interrupted to tell Pattie that he loved her, which made her shy. He was smartly dressed and had a healthy head of white hair, just like Norman. Muriel leant in and asked where her bicycle was. In the chair opposite, Francis repeatedly sang a garbled version of *"There'll be Blue Birds Over the White Cliffs of Dover."* I wondered what the 'noisy room' was like.

I fed her tea through a baby cup. It was tepid and weak, there was no chance that this cup of tea would ever fix anything. I told her the complete story of how she got to this point, just in case somewhere in her mind she needed to know. I needed her to know. Residents listened in as I read chapters of her book out loud. I learnt that the comatose lady in the adjacent seat was a prima ballerina and the man opposite, babbling to a teddy bear, was a lawyer. Suddenly

I realised that Alzheimer's could affect anyone, not just my mother. Every family struggled with the helplessness of the disease, not just us. In an instant I stopped feeling sorry for myself or angry with God.

Christianne, Scott, and Benjamin joined me on my last visit to the home. We took Pattie her favourite Jelly Babies and sat on footstools around her chair, chatting about anything and everything that would hide the sadness of my looming farewell. Henry lightened the mood by professing his undying love for us all and Lily pushed past with her Zimmer frame laughing as my mother was hoisted into the dining room for lunch. We huddled protectively around Pattie and made a fuss of the liquidised roast beef that she was about to be spoon fed. While Pattie received another mouthful, Christianne waved hello to Mary who was sitting in a wheelchair alone at the next table. Mary didn't respond, she was too distracted smiling lovingly at Scott and Ben like they were her own grandchildren. She looked like the quintessential English rose and her vintage bangs of snow-white hair fell on either side of her porcelain rosy-cheeked face. The pearls around her neck fell over a beige Cashmere cardigan and diamond earrings sparkled like her bright blue eyes. I felt uncomfortable fussing over Pattie while Mary sat unattended and walked over to ask if she would like to join us. Her eyes narrowed and her ruby red lips curled into a snarl.

"F...off!" She screamed.

I burst into tears, but Mary was so foul that I started laughing uncontrollably at the incredulity of it all and set Pattie and Christianne off as well as the boys. It was contagious and soon enough the carers and diners were all roaring with laughter while Mary continued to expel foul language relentlessly throughout lunch. By the time bloody

Mary was wheeled out of the dining room our cheeks were burning.

I kissed Pattie goodbye while she was distracted with apple pie and custard pudding. From the car park I watched her being hoisted past the window to the lounge and thought she gave me a smile.

Back on the veranda in Zimbabwe I waited for Christianne's weekly skype call and opened my laptop on the last pages of this book. Scruffy lay on my lap and Muffin was chewing a squeaky toy in her basket. It was another beautiful morning, and the garden was full of life. Wood hoopoes scratched through the palm fronds searching for insects and a sunbird tapped its reflection in the window, chirping loudly at the handsomeness of its image. A woodpecker pecked at the bottlebrush tree and yellow and white butterflies fluttered around the garden beds, kissing lavender flowers.

My heart skipped a beat again when Pattie's face appeared on the Skype screen. Slumped sideways in her chair, she was unresponsive to my rambling stories about the week's events, but her carers leant in and waved hello to me. My prayers had been answered; they were kind to my mother. She was in the 'noisy room' and slept most of the day. Stimulation came from the movie *Paint Your Wagon* blasting out from the television and a small lovebird chirping from inside a cage. Sufferers in early stages of the disease trudged past in disgust, disbelieving they would ever get as bad. Muriel flashed past the screen a few times, still searching for her bicycle. Christianne rubbed cream gently onto Pattie's face and placed a newspaper on her lap. Pattie leant forward for a better look at photographs of the Royal family but didn't have the strength to hold her position for long and slumped back into the chair. Very few of her characteristics had survived the disease but when I fed her a Jelly Baby and Christianne gave her a good squirt of

Chanel No 5, there it was, her smile. Her enduring, radiant, trademark smile.

The helplessness of Alzheimer's disease had deeply affected me and a book that I started years ago in the beauty of the Ume River had helped me heal. By putting my mother's story in black and white, I made sure the disease that killed her would never define her life. It was there for all to read and for me to remember, in case I too, forgot.

"Hildah, God is there!" I shouted. "My book is finished!"

"Madam, it must be a long story," she yelled, giving Scruffy a fright. "Stop it Scruffy it's me Hildah."

Pattie died in 2017, six years after her diagnosis. It had been a long goodbye and Christianne spent the last 10 days by her side. I didn't cry at the funeral nor when I read her eulogy: I thought at the time that I had no tears left, but I was wrong, they caught up with me later.

My mother was born in Canada and died in England. In between she lived a colourful life in Africa filling this book with *Green Stamps for Heaven*. I imagined her arm in arm with Norman, tossing her crutches aside and running towards Pope John Paul II in his papal coloured balaclava, shouting "It's me again, Pattie, now let me tell you a story!"

2009 Pattie and Norman in Dorset

2004 Vicki in Harare

Circa 1917 Francis Stein driving in London

1926 John Patrick and Veronica in Canada

1945 Pattie holding Bill the dog, Bin, Maureen, Angela and Margaret in Devon

1952 Ken and Pattie in Paris

1961 Bambo Jomba mobile puppet theatre in Zomba

1961 Pattie with a child after puppeteering in Zomba

1970 Christianne, Pattie and Elisabeth in Quorn Ave, Salisbury, Rhodesia

1970 Christianne, Pattie and Elisabeth with Ringo Star and Kelly in Rhodesia

1970 Miracle Babies - YOU Magazine

1988 Pattie with Pope John Paul II at Harare Catholic Cathedral

www.ingramcontent.com/pod-product-compliance
Lightning Source LLC
Chambersburg PA
CBHW030255100526
44590CB00012B/407